Explore
the Bible ®

Let the Word dwell in you.

SUBJECT HEADING: BIBLE. O.T. PSALMS—STUDY AND TEACHING / GOD / SPIRITUAL LIFE

ERIC GEIGER
Vice President, LifeWay Resources

MICHAEL KELLY
Director, Groups Ministry

ROBERT SMITH JR.
General Editor

SAM HOUSE
Content Editor

With *Explore the Bible*, groups can expect to engage Scripture in its proper context and be better prepared to live it out in their own context. These book-by-book studies will help participants—

> grow in their love for Scripture;

> gain new knowledge about what the Bible teaches;

> develop biblical disciplines;

> internalize the Word in a way that transforms their lives.

Send questions/comments to: Content Editor, *Explore the Bible: Small-Group Study;* One LifeWay Plaza; Nashville, TN 37234-0152.

Printed in the United States of America

For ordering or inquiries visit *lifeway.com;* write to LifeWay Small Groups; One LifeWay Plaza; Nashville, TN 37234-0152; or call toll free 800.458.2772.

We believe that the Bible has God for its author; salvation for its end; and truth, without any mixture of error, for its matter and that all Scripture is totally true and trustworthy. To review LifeWay's doctrinal guideline, please visit *lifeway.com/doctrinalguideline.*

Scripture quotations are taken from the Christian Standard Bible®, Copyright © 2017 by Holman Bible Publishers®. Used by permission. Christian Standard Bible® and CSB® are federally registered trademarks of Holman Bible Publishers.

Session 1 quotation: Charles H. Spurgeon, *The Treasury of David: Spurgeon's Classic Work on the Psalms,* abr. David O. Fuller (Grand Rapids, MI: Kregel, 1968), 13. Session 2 quotation: Corrie Ten Boom, as quoted on Thinkexist.com [online, cited 5 January 2017]. Available from the Internet: *thinkexist.com.* Session 3 quotation: A. W. Tozer, *The Counselor,* rev. ed. (Chicago: Moody, 1993). Session 4 quotation: C. S. Lewis, *The Problem of Pain* (New York: HarperOne, 1996), 46. Session 5 quotation: Matthew Henry, *Matthew Henry's Concise Commentary on the Whole Bible* (Nashville: Thomas Nelson, 2003). Session 6 quotation: Elisabeth Elliot, *Passion and Purity: Learning to Bring Your Love Life Under Christ's Control* (Grand Rapids, MI: Revell, 2002), 85.

 Connect

 @ExploreTheBible

 facebook.com/ExploreTheBible

 lifeway.com/ExploreTheBible

 ministrygrid.com/web/ExploreTheBible

❯ ABOUT THIS STUDY

Sometimes when we read the Bible, it seems as if our lives are worlds apart from those depicted on the pages of Scripture. It's easy to ponder, sometimes with guilt and secrecy in our hearts, whether the Bible is relevant to our feelings, thoughts, struggles, or circumstances.

This study of the Book of Psalms holds good news for you. A psalmist has likely written about whatever feelings you might experience in any situation in which you find yourself. These lessons speak to those who are soaring on the heights of spiritual growth and to those who are in the depths of spiritual weakness. It legitimizes the feelings of those seeking God's recompense for persecutors and those seeking forgiveness for having done wrong to others. It teaches lessons for dealing with the perils or the successes of life with great grace, patience, and faith while extolling the loving-kindness of our God, who is always worthy of praise.

No matter what you're experiencing in life, this journey through the Book of Psalms is for you. If you earnestly apply its lessons, it will provide inspiration and godly wisdom as you seek to walk the narrow path surrounded by distractions from your devotion to God, challenges to your faith, and contemporary philosophies that aim to compete with biblical truth.

The **Explore the Bible** series will help you know and apply the encouraging and empowering truth of God's Word. Each session is organized in the following way.

UNDERSTAND THE CONTEXT: This page explains the original context of each passage and begins relating the primary themes to your life today.

EXPLORE THE TEXT: These pages walk you through Scripture, providing helpful commentary and encouraging thoughtful interaction with God through His Word.

OBEY THE TEXT: This page helps you apply the truths you've explored. It's not enough to know what the Bible says. God's Word has the power to change your life.

LEADER GUIDE: This final section provides optional discussion starters and suggested questions to help anyone lead a group in reviewing each section of the personal study.

For helps on how to use *Explore the Bible*, tips on how to better lead groups, or additional ideas for leading, visit: **ministrygrid.com/web/ExploreTheBible.**

❯ GROUP COMMITMENT

As you begin this study, it's important that everyone agrees to key group values. Clearly establishing the purpose of your time together will foster healthy expectations and help ease any uncertainties. The goal is to ensure that everyone has a positive experience leading to spiritual growth and true community. Initial each value as you discuss the following with your group.

❏ PRIORITY

Life is busy, but we value this time with one another and with God's Word. We choose to make being together a priority.

❏ PARTICIPATION

We're a group. Everyone is encouraged to participate. No one dominates.

❏ RESPECT

Everyone is given the right to his or her own opinions. All questions are encouraged and respected.

❏ TRUST

Each person humbly seeks truth through time in prayer and in the Bible. We trust God as the loving authority in our lives.

❏ CONFIDENTIALITY

Anything said in our meetings is never repeated outside the group without the permission of everyone involved. This commitment is vital in creating an environment of trust and openness.

❏ SUPPORT

Everyone can count on anyone in this group. Permission is given to call on one another at any time, especially in times of crisis. The group provides care for every member.

❏ ACCOUNTABILITY

We agree to let the members of our group hold us accountable to commitments we make in the loving ways we decide on. Questions are always welcome. Unsolicited advice, however, isn't permitted.

_____   _____

I agree to all the commitments.   Date

❯ GENERAL EDITOR

 **Dr. Robert Smith Jr.** serves as the Charles T. Carter Baptist chair of divinity and professor of Christian preaching at Beeson Divinity School in Birmingham, Alabama. He's the author of *Doctrine that Dances: Bring Doctrinal Preaching and Teaching to Life*.

› CONTENTS

THE PATH

Believers should embrace godly wisdom because obedience to God's Word is the path of true life.

ABOUT THE BOOK OF PSALMS

The Book of Psalms displays a broad range of content and style. New Testament writers quoted from Psalms and Isaiah more than any other Old Testament book. Paul stated that the early church sang psalms in their worship (see Eph. 5:19).

Writer. Numerous people wrote the psalms. The writers of some are unknown. Many psalms have superscriptions with names such as David, Moses, Asaph, Korah, and Solomon. However, the Hebrew preposition *of* may mean "by," "for," "about," or "concerning." Thus, "a psalm of David" or "a Davidic psalm" may mean David wrote the text, but in a few cases it may mean something else. The sons of Korah were descendants of the Levite who died for rebelling against Moses and Aaron (see Num. 26:10-11). Some served as singers and musicians in the temple choir. Heman was the founder of the choir during the monarchy of David. Asaph and Jeuthum were choir directors.

Date. Each psalm must be dated independently. The psalms were written, used, and collected over the entire period of Israel's history. They were the result of both personal and national experiences. The Book of Psalms was in its present form by the fourth century B.C.

Titles. All but 34 of the psalms have individual titles. Although these titles are very ancient, many scholars conclude that they were likely added after the poems were written. Nonetheless, it's very unlikely that later scribes would have inserted titles for psalms that didn't clearly reflect the situation described in the title.

Outline. Since ancient times Psalms has been divided into five books, presumably corresponding to the five books of the Law. Each division ends in a doxology. Psalm 1 serves as an introduction to the Book of Psalms, Psalm 150 as the conclusion.

Types. Identifying the type of psalm can give you insight into its original use and context. Types of psalms include lament, thanksgiving, hymn, royal, enthronement, penitential, and wisdom.

"WHEN MEN ARE LIVING IN SIN, THEY GO FROM BAD TO WORSE. AT FIRST THEY MERELY *WALK* IN THE COUNSEL OF THE CARELESS AND UNGODLY, WHO FORGET GOD ... BUT AFTER THAT, THEY BECOME HABITUATED TO EVIL, AND THEY *STAND* IN THE WAY OF OPEN SINNERS WHO WILLFULLY VIOLATE GOD'S COMMANDMENTS."
—*Charles H. Spurgeon*

where am I being formed by things around me?

› PSALM 1

Think About It

Observe the variety of images employed in Psalm 1. What do these assorted, real-life sketches suggest about the importance of making correct choices?

Notice the number of times the word wicked occurs in Psalm 1. Why do you think the writer repeated this term so many times?

1 How happy is the one who does not
walk in the advice of the wicked
or _stand_ in the pathway with sinners
or _sit_ in the company of mockers!
2 Instead, his delight is in the LORD's instruction,
and he meditates on it day and night.
3 He is like a tree planted beside flowing streams
that bears its fruit in its season
and whose leaf does not wither.
Whatever he does prospers.
4 The wicked are not like this;
instead, they are like chaff that the wind blows away.
5 Therefore the wicked will not stand up in the judgment,
nor sinners in the assembly of the righteous.
6 For the LORD watches over the way of the righteous,
but the way of the wicked leads to ruin.

 Many psalms were intended to be sung. Go to the leader helps at *lifeway.com/explorethebible* to hear some of these psalms set to music and to download free worship arrangements of them.

The raw volitile emotions that David expresses and vocalizes to God AND can still be honoring Him.

❯ UNDERSTAND THE CONTEXT

USE THE FOLLOWING PAGES TO PREPARE FOR YOUR GROUP TIME.

Psalm 1 is commonly classified as a wisdom psalm. *Wisdom* may be defined as "the appropriate application of knowledge." For example, understanding that a light socket conducts electricity is knowledge. Wisdom is keeping one's finger out of the socket. On the other hand, screwing a light bulb into the socket in order to illuminate the darkness shows an even higher form of wisdom. Wisdom psalms present examples of human behavior to demonstrate that some behaviors are wise and some are foolish. These examples are intended to point readers to choices that please God. Wisdom psalms tend to be proverbial. Indeed, many of the ideas in this psalm have parallels in the Book of Proverbs.

Psalm 1 must be viewed in relation to the entire Book of Psalms. This first psalm serves as an introduction to the entire psalter. In like manner, Psalm 150 functions as the conclusion to the book. In Psalm 1 the righteous are blessed by God, and in Psalm 150 the righteous bless God. Psalm 1 describes what God does for His people, and Psalm 150 instructs God's people to bless God.

Psalm 1 easily divides into two parts: the path of life (see vv. 1-3) and the path of death (see vv. 4-6). The two lifestyles are contrasted in the first two verses. Then in verses 3-4 the nature and value of each lifestyle are sketched with a botanical analogy. The last two verses then disclose the ultimate fate of each lifestyle.

❯ EXPLORE THE TEXT

THE PATH OF LIFE (Psalm 1:1-3)

¹How happy is the one who does not walk in the advice of the wicked or stand in the pathway with sinners or sit in the company of mockers!

The Book of Psalms reveals much about how to have a blessed or happy life. The word *happy* is translated "blessed" in some translations (KJV, ESV, NIV). The term is best understood as the sense of joy, blessedness, or contentment of those who faithfully walk in a right relationship with God. The word essentially points to the best possible life an individual can achieve and occurs at least 20 times in the Book of Psalms.

Take note in Psalm 1:1 of the progressive action from walking to standing to sitting. In this image of life as a journey down a path, a traveler stops to listen to the banter of bystanders. The unsuspecting journeyer soon joins the conversation and eventually takes a seat among these gabbers. In contrast, the traveler in verse 1 doesn't do these things. He doesn't stop, stand, or become one of the wicked.

A wicked person is someone who is corrupt in his or her heart. Sinners continuously practice sin. Mockers scoff at God. The word *walk* refers to the decisions a person makes in life. The word *stand* refers to a person's commitments, and sitting represents a person's attitudes and the disposition of his or her heart.

This verse warns the reader that each step is a choice. The psalm encourages readers to avoid that choice. Don't be influenced by the wicked. Refuse to walk down the sinful path. Don't align yourself with those who scoff at what is holy. The psalmist wasn't offering a method for avoiding the wicked. The psalmist's words serve as a warning to be careful about our close associations.

²Instead, his delight is in the LORD's instruction, and he meditates on it day and night.

If certain behaviors must be avoided in order to attain biblical happiness, then what conduct is acceptable? The answer isn't a catalog of activities but dependence on a single source that will produce appropriate behavior in any situation. The source is "the LORD's instruction," literally "Yahweh's law." This phrase is synonymous with Scripture. Scripture transforms the nature of those who delight in it. Such people read the Bible because they hunger for God. They eagerly absorb its instructions and constantly seek to abide by them.

Biblical meditation isn't related to Eastern religions or transcendental meditation. The Hebrew verb means "to read or repeat Scripture in an audible whisper." The command to meditate on it day and night doesn't mean God expects people to read the Bible 24 hours a day, seven days a week. However, it does mean that the actions of the righteous are steered by the truths of Scripture at all times. God's Word has become an integral part of their thinking.

³He is like a tree planted beside flowing streams that bears its fruit in its season and whose leaf does not wither. Whatever he does prospers.

The psalmist compared the person who follows God's counsel to a productive tree planted near a river or irrigation canal. The verb *planted* reveals that the tree didn't sprout in this location by chance. God set it in this place. The analogy points to the Bible as God's resource for living in a manner that keeps a person right with Him.

The person who follows the counsel of God's Word will flourish and produce fruit. Therefore, God's Word supplies everything necessary for living a fruitful and rewarding life. The phrase "Whatever he does prospers" doesn't guarantee financial prosperity or career advancement. Rather, because this person follows the counsel of God's Word, his or her ambition is to glorify God, not to obtain monetary or personal reward.

What's the godly fruit that God desires for His followers to produce? How can worldly wisdom hinder growth? How does reading the Bible nurture the development of this godly fruit?

THE PATH OF DEATH (Psalm 1:4-5)

⁴The wicked are not like this; instead, they are like chaff that the wind blows away.

The psalmist pointed out that the wicked are like worthless chaff that the wind blows away. The words "not like this" are emphatic in the Hebrew text. The wicked are the opposite of all that was said about the righteous in the previous three verses.

In ancient Israel harvested grain stalks were laid out to dry, commonly in a shallow pit cut in the stone bedrock of a hilltop. After the stalks dried, the grain was beaten on the rock surface either with a large stone or with the hoofs of animals walking on the grain. In the evening the wind normally blew harder across the hill. At that time the farmer used a winnowing fork to toss the beaten crop up into the evening breeze. The heavy kernels of grain dropped back onto the threshing floor, while the chaff was blown away.

⁵Therefore the wicked will not stand up in the judgment, nor sinners in the assembly of the righteous.

Listening to the deceptive advice of the wicked leads to instability and destruction. The psalmist warned his readers that the wicked face sure judgment and eternal separation from God's righteous people. When the wicked are brought before the Almighty in judgment, they will be unable to defend the choices that produced their lifestyle. God's verdict will result in eternal separation from Him.

How should God's warning about the future of the wicked affect you? How should you feel? What should you do?

BIBLE SKILL
Use other Scriptures to help understand a Bible passage.

The psalmist wasn't the only one to emphasize the importance of life choices. Compare Psalm 1 with Deuteronomy 30:19-20 and Matthew 7:24-27. How are these passages similar? What common themes are found in all three passages? Record a summary statement of the teachings found in all three passages.

THE CONCLUSION (Psalm 1:6)

⁶**For the LORD watches over the way of the righteous, but the way of the wicked leads to ruin.**

"The LORD watches over the way of the righteous" stresses that God's knowledge of the righteous is a present reality. The verb itself means "to know through experience." God's knowledge of His people is knowledge that's derived by walking with His people.

The word LORD is the Hebrew Yahweh. This is the name God used in His covenant with Israel and therefore indicates that the relationship is an intimate one. The intimacy of God's knowledge guarantees His presence to secure His people. Believers can live with confidence, knowing that God guarantees His protection to the obedient.

The righteous are individuals who are right with God. Their way is a lifestyle of faith. Faith isn't merely saying words but is a trust that produces obedient acts. However, the lifestyle of the ungodly ultimately "leads to ruin."

What does this verse teach about the security of those who follow God? How does this security affect our behavior?

❯ OBEY THE TEXT

- Fulfillment in life is found through faithful obedience to God and His Word.

- Falling for the deceptive advice of the wicked leads to instability, worthlessness, and destruction.

- Believers can live with confidence, knowing that God guarantees His protection to the obedient.

What's the role of the Bible in your life? How much time do you spend reading and studying the Bible on a weekly basis? What actions can you take to increase that time?

As a group, list ways ungodliness is promoted in our world today. How can your Bible-study group help one another avoid the influence of these sins?

What are some situations in your life in which godly living is difficult? How do you determine what God wants you to do in these situations? What are some Bible verses that can give you confidence to do what God wants?

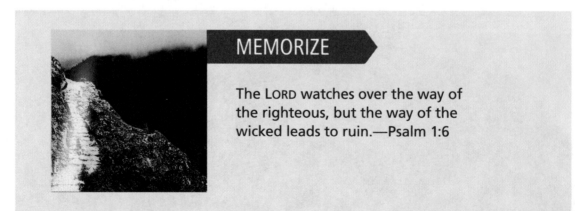

MEMORIZE

The LORD watches over the way of the righteous, but the way of the wicked leads to ruin.—Psalm 1:6

USE THE SPACE PROVIDED TO MAKE OBSERVATIONS AND RECORD PRAYER REQUESTS DURING THE GROUP EXPERIENCE FOR THIS SESSION.

MY THOUGHTS

Record insights and questions from the group experience.

MY RESPONSE

Note specific ways you'll put into practice the truth explored this week.

MY PRAYERS

List specific prayer needs and answers to remember this week.

Abigail's health
SLI homework for Michelle

THE SHEPHERD

God can be trusted because He's always good.

⟩ UNDERSTAND THE CONTEXT

USE THE FOLLOWING PAGES TO PREPARE FOR YOUR GROUP TIME.

David was a shepherd in his youth (see 1 Sam. 16:11). As a shepherd, he would have spent long hours alone with his father's sheep. Sheep not only provided food and wool for the family, but they were also a measure of family wealth. Therefore, a shepherd's responsibility for the sheep's welfare directly affected the family's survival and status. The wilderness of Judah could be an inhospitable place for sheep. Water and grass were scarce. Consequently, David would have frequently moved his flocks to new locations to feed and water them satisfactorily. He fought predators such as bears and lions in order to protect his sheep (see 17:34-37).

During David's night watch over his flocks, he would have had the opportunity to gaze at the infinite stars twinkling overhead. Instead of feeling insignificant in the vastness of the universe, he recognized that God had given humanity a special role in creation. This outward paradox elicited great praise for the Lord from David (see Ps. 8).

In Psalm 23 David depicted his relationship with God in terms of a shepherd and his sheep. He drew from his own experience of what his sheep needed and what he offered them. Just as David supplied nourishment, protection, and shelter for his sheep, God provided direction, security, and care for him.

Like numerous other psalms, Psalm 23 is identified as Davidic. The Hebrew title is ambiguous. It can mean "written by," "belonging to," "about," or "for," so this title doesn't prove David was the author. However, David was also a musician (see 1 Sam. 16:18-23), and the content of this psalm easily fits David's life experience. Therefore, although we can't be absolutely certain, David was likely the writer. Later, others borrowed his metaphor and identified the Lord as the Shepherd of Israel (see Ps. 80:1; Isa. 40:11; Ezek. 34:11-16). Jesus also used this image to depict His relationship with His followers (see John 10:1-21). He described the Good Shepherd as giving His life to prevent harm to His sheep. His sheep have an intimate relationship with the Good Shepherd, and they respond to His voice. God is our personal Shepherd, just as He was for David.

> "NEVER BE AFRAID TO TRUST AN UNKNOWN FUTURE TO A KNOWN GOD."
> —*Corrie Ten Boom*

⟩ PSALM 23

Think About It

Circle the first-person pronouns. What do these suggest about the psalmist's view of God?

Notice the shift from the pronoun he in verses 2-3 to you in verses 4-5. Why do you think this shift is important?

1 The LORD is my shepherd;
I have what I need.
2 He lets me lie down in green pastures;
he leads me beside quiet waters.
3 He renews my life;
he leads me along the right paths
for his name's sake.
4 Even when I go through the darkest valley,
I fear no danger,
for you are with me;
your rod and your staff—they comfort me.
5 You prepare a table before me
in the presence of my enemies;
you anoint my head with oil;
my cup overflows.
6 Only goodness and faithful love will pursue
me all the days of my life,
and I will dwell in the house of the LORD
as long as I live.

Movement of God towards me, His sheep.

Many psalms were intended to be sung. Go to the leader helps at *lifeway.com/explorethebible* to hear some of these psalms set to music and to download free worship arrangements of them.

› EXPLORE THE TEXT

THE SHEPHERD PROVIDES (Psalm 23:1-3)

¹The LORD is my shepherd; I have what I need.

Whenever LORD is printed in capital letters in the Old Testament, the term denotes the covenant name of Israel's God, Yahweh (or Jehovah). God's name is more than a label for identification. It communicates His nature and character. God is a personal being. Though He certainly isn't human, figurative language describing God in human terms reveals a profound reality that abstract terminology often can't portray. The Lord is a God who desires an intimate, personal relationship with people. He used this name when He entered a covenant relationship with Israel (see Ex. 20:2).

In the Hebrew text of this verse, "the LORD" is emphatic. The covenant God of Israel was David's shepherd. The relationship between the Shepherd and His sheep is personal. The pronoun *my* conveys the intimate nature of David's relationship with God. It also implies that God can become the reader's Shepherd as well. Jesus described Himself as our Shepherd if we're His followers (see John 10:14). The Good Shepherd knows us, and we know Him.

The primary function of a shepherd is care. Docile sheep can't care for themselves. They depend on the shepherd for protection, food, water, and shelter. These needs demand the physical presence of the shepherd at all times. Because the Lord is our shepherd, anxiety about our needs isn't appropriate. God will take care of us. "I have what I need" doesn't mean believers will have every material, financial, and physical benefit we want. We won't. Just as a shepherd owns his sheep and uses them for his benefit, Christ is the believer's Lord. We exist to serve Him. Therefore, our Shepherd provides us with everything we require to accomplish the tasks He assigns to us.

²He lets me lie down in green pastures; he leads me beside quiet waters.

In this verse the psalmist emphasized the shepherd's care for the physical needs of his sheep. In the Hebrew text the verb translated "He lets me lie down" stresses God's role. He makes His flock lie down in the noonday heat. But the action involves more than simply reclining. It incorporates the provisions of the location. A green pasture is a place where the sheep can eat and then safely lie down to rest when full and satisfied. The adjective *green* denotes that the field has tender young sprouts, the sheep's preferred meal. God's involvement in our lives includes the provision of nourishment, safety, and rest.

The verb *leads* suggests gentle guidance. A good shepherd leads his flock rather than driving it. Sheep require water daily because of the climate in the Middle East. However, sheep are afraid of flowing water. Therefore, the shepherd must provide quiet waters for them to drink, and his sheep instinctively follow him there.

What are some ways God provides safety and the necessities of life? What prevents people from recognizing His involvement in providing these things?

³He renews my life; he leads me along the right paths for his name's sake.

"He renews my life" recalls the shepherd's bringing back the straying sheep. Regrettably, all Christians wander away from God on occasion. In doing so, we expose ourselves to many dangers. Fortunately, when we stray, God seeks to bring us back into His fold. Jesus compared God to a shepherd who lost 1 sheep. This shepherd left 99 other sheep to search for the one that strayed (see Matt. 18:12-14).

The idea of the shepherd as a leader is repeated. In order to reach safe pastures, the flocks must move. The shepherd selects the route of travel. It's along "the right paths"—safe paths that are free from dangers. This doesn't mean the path is without peril but that God's presence eliminates our fear. God guides His followers down the right paths "for his name's sake"—to uphold His own reputation. In Hebrew thinking, someone's name reflected his or her character. When God's people do right, they vindicate God's character.

David drew metaphors from his life experience. How would you convey the biblical truth in these verses, using contemporary analogies from your own life experience?

THE SHEPHERD GUARDS *(Psalm 23:4)*

⁴Even when I go through the darkest valley, I fear no danger, for you are with me; your rod and your staff—they comfort me.

In this verse the psalmist ceased to write about God and began to speak to God. David characterized God as guarding His sheep, walking with them when they face challenges. Following the right path sometimes leads through dangerous sites. "The darkest valley" describes an extreme danger that seems life-threatening. Predators lurk in the dark shadows of the valley's rocky slopes. It's there that one's footing is most precarious. Even though the path goes into a place of danger, there's no need to fear, because the Good Shepherd is present with His sheep. The Good Shepherd is also the light, and the light illuminates the darkness (see John 1:5).

The rod and the staff describe the shepherd's crook. This tool can be employed as a club. With it the shepherd defends his sheep. He may also use it as a stick on which to rest himself. He uses the hook at one end to seize the legs of the sheep that are prone to run. Thus, the rod and the staff can be used to resist danger that threatens the flock or to prevent sheep from wandering into danger. A good shepherd would risk his life to protect his flock. Jesus said, "I am the good shepherd. The good shepherd lays down his life for the sheep" (John 10:11). He gave His life, but He also took it back up just as He promised (see vv. 17-18). Now He's alive and present with His sheep. His presence guards their path even in the most hostile circumstances.

How do the sheep express trust in the shepherd? In what ways is obedience a function of trust?

THE SHEPHERD HOSTS *(Psalm 23:5-6)*

⁵You prepare a table before me in the presence of my enemies; you anoint my head with oil; my cup overflows.

David reminded his readers that God serves as a gracious host to His sheep, offering them protection, healing, and shelter. Some Bible scholars think the metaphor here changes from a shepherd to a dinner host. The ancient Jewish banquet was a public event. Although invited guests might be seated at the table, anybody could come into the dining room, stand around, and watch the proceedings. Enemies were anyone who sought to cause discomfort and anguish. Other scholars continue to see the metaphor of a shepherd and his sheep. In that case the table refers to a strip of leather laid out on the ground by the shepherd when grazing wasn't available. He spread fodder out on it for the sheep to eat. Enemies, in this case, were the numerous predators and dangers of the region. In either case the analogy indicates that God's people are never completely removed from trouble. However, God is always present to help them.

Pouring oil on the head was an act of honor. In the ancient Middle East, ointments and perfumes were customarily poured on certain guests at banquets. Shepherds also carried flasks of oil to doctor their sheep. Sheep's faces were routinely cut and scratched while foraging in thorny areas.

The cup is frequently used in a figurative sense in Scripture. Here it denotes God's provision and protection. The supply in the cup exceeds what the guest needs. Remember, the security is in His presence, not in the material goods He furnishes.

⁶Only goodness and faithful love will pursue me all the days of my life, and I will dwell in the house of the LORD as long as I live.

The word *only* reflects a deep belief that a godly person will always prevail. No crisis will overpower and destroy a person who trusts God to supply his or her needs. God desires a personal relationship in which we depend on Him for comfort and support during times of crisis. An even stronger bond with Him is forged by our dependence on Him during such troubles.

The psalmist identified two attributes of God that ensure God's people will prevail. First is His goodness. The Hebrew term denotes that which is desirable and beneficial. Here it has a sense of superior quality. Thus, it describes God's nature and actions working for the welfare of His people. His faithful love, the second quality the psalmist named, is an expression of God's relationship with His people. The Hebrew term is one of the most difficult to translate into English. The word always appears in the context of a covenant relationship, usually that of Yahweh and Israel. It signifies the conduct expected of parties in a covenant relationship and includes their loyalty to its terms. Therefore, it denotes faithfulness to a covenant. However, that loyalty is born from love. Therefore, the term emphasizes Yahweh's love for His covenant people.

The psalmist's absolute confidence in God is expressed in the words "I will dwell in the house of the LORD as long as I live." The temple hadn't been constructed in David's lifetime, so the house of the Lord represents the place where God dwells with His people. No structure erected by humanity can contain God (see Isa. 66:1-2). He's greater than His creation. Hence, the psalmist asserted that he would always live in God's presence.

What characteristics of God give confidence in times of trouble and in times of prosperity? How do verses 5-6 encourage a person who faces a time of trouble? How do these verses bring perspective for a person who experiences a time of prosperity?

❯ OBEY THE TEXT

- Believers can be confident that God provides for all their needs.

- We can find comfort in knowing that God promises His presence in every life experience.

- Believers can be thankful for God's eternal care for them.

Examine the stressors in your life, looking for any areas that reflect a greater need to trust God and His provision for you. Ask God to help you trust Him to provide for your needs (be specific). Record your prayer below.

Sometimes when we're overwhelmed by a situation, it becomes difficult to discern God's provisions. Enlist your Bible-study group to analyze some of one another's troublesome times. Determine practical ways to incorporate mutual support into the life of your Bible-study group.

Make an inventory of the essentials you need to survive. In what ways has God supplied each of these? Record the name of one person with whom you can share ways God provides for you.

MEMORIZE

The LORD is my shepherd; I have what I need.—Psalm 23:1

USE THE SPACE PROVIDED TO MAKE OBSERVATIONS AND RECORD PRAYER REQUESTS DURING THE GROUP EXPERIENCE FOR THIS SESSION.

MY THOUGHTS

Record insights and questions from the group experience.

_____

_____

_____

_____

_____

_____

MY RESPONSE

Note specific ways you'll put into practice the truth explored this week.

_____

_____

_____

_____

_____

MY PRAYERS

List specific prayer needs and answers to remember this week.

Who is walking through a valley right now
that I can share my overflowing cup
from the Lord / Shepherds provision in
my own life.

_____

_____

THE PRESENCE

Security is found in the assurance of God's presence.

❯ UNDERSTAND THE CONTEXT

USE THE FOLLOWING PAGES TO PREPARE FOR YOUR GROUP TIME.

According to its title, Psalm 84 is a psalm of the sons of Korah. The Korahites were gatekeepers in the temple and likely also served as musicians. Eleven psalms are connected to them. The note that this psalm is for the choir director supports the idea that it was used in temple worship. The meaning of the notation "on the Gittith," however, is unclear.

What's undeniable is the writer's yearning to be at the temple in Jerusalem. This longing grew from the role of the temple under the old covenant. The heart of the temple was the holy of holies. The only furnishing in this room was the ark of the covenant. God was said to be enthroned above its cherubim (see 2 Sam. 6:2; Ps. 80:1). Yet only once a year did anyone enter this most sacred space. On the Day of Atonement the high priest went inside alone. Nevertheless, because God's people recognized the holy of holies as God's throne, the temple represented the invisible presence of God on earth. To enter the temple was to be in His presence and to fellowship with Him.

Furthermore, the temple was designated in the law as the prescribed site for performing the mandatory and voluntary offerings. Though each had distinct purposes, they all functioned as elements employed to worship the one true God.

As Jesus died on the cross, the veil that separated the holy of holies from the rest of the temple was torn from top to bottom. In that act God invited all people to approach Him boldly through the blood of Jesus (see Heb. 10:19-22). Moreover, under the new covenant inaugurated by Christ's blood, God is permanently present within every believer through the indwelling Holy Spirit.

> "I WANT THE PRESENCE OF GOD HIMSELF, OR I DON'T WANT ANYTHING AT ALL TO DO WITH RELIGION. YOU WOULD NEVER GET ME INTERESTED IN THE OLD MAIDS' SOCIAL CLUB WITH A LITTLE BIT OF CHRISTIANITY THROWN IN TO GIVE IT RESPECTABILITY. I WANT ALL THAT GOD HAS, OR I DON'T WANT ANY."
>
> —A. W. Tozer

❯ PSALM 84

Think About It

Note the titles and designations used for God. Identify the title or designation used the most. What are some implications of its repetition?

Identify things the psalmist named that produce happiness. How did these things influence the decisions the psalmist made?

1 How lovely is your dwelling place,
LORD of Armies.
2 I long and yearn
for the courts of the LORD;
my heart and flesh cry out for the living God.
3 Even a sparrow finds a home,
and a swallow, a nest for herself
where she places her young—
near your altars, LORD of Armies,
my King and my God.
4 How happy are those who reside in your house,
who praise you continually.
5 Happy are the people whose strength is in you,
whose hearts are set on pilgrimage.
6 As they pass through the Valley of Baca,
they make it a source of spring water;
even the autumn rain will cover it with blessings.
7 They go from strength to strength;
each appears before God in Zion.
8 LORD God of Armies, hear my prayer;
listen, God of Jacob.
9 Consider our shield, God;
look on the face of your anointed one.
10 Better a day in your courts
than a thousand anywhere else.
I would rather stand at the threshold of the house of my God
than live in the tents of wicked people.
11 For the LORD God is a sun and shield.
The LORD grants favor and honor;
he does not withhold the good
from those who live with integrity.
12 Happy is the person who trusts in you,
LORD of Armies!

 Many psalms were intended to be sung. Go to the leader helps at *lifeway.com/explorethebible* to hear some of these psalms set to music and to download free worship arrangements of them.

❯ EXPLORE THE TEXT

THE PASSION *(Psalm 84:1-4)*

¹How lovely is your dwelling place, LORD of Armies.

This psalm depicts a pilgrim going to the temple. The writer referred to the temple as God's dwelling place. The Hebrew word is the plural form of *tabernacle*, the portable structure fabricated during Israel's exodus from Egypt. This word accentuates the nearness of God inside the temple precincts. Speaking directly to God, the psalmist expressed his desire to be in the temple. This initial statement unveils almost a giddy reaction as he came near the sacred structure.

Yet the pilgrim couldn't escape the awesome nature of God. He addressed God as LORD of Armies. LORD is God's personal name, Yahweh. It's compounded with a military term for *armies*. In its early uses in Israel's history, this title affirmed Yahweh as the true commander of Israel's army. However, this meaning doesn't fully account for all of the term's usages in Scripture. Early in its history Israel acknowledged that God likewise commanded an angelic army. Later the word was also coupled with *heaven* (see 2 Kings 17:16) to denote God's authority over the heavenly bodies. Thus, LORD of Armies is an exalted title that expresses divine sovereignty. God commands.

²I long and yearn for the courts of the LORD; my heart and flesh cry out for the living God.

The psalmist employed two intense verbs to express his unquenchable craving to stand inside the temple. His yearning wasn't for the physical facility but for entrance into God's presence. He knew the purpose of the temple was to worship God.

The word *living* denotes physical life. When used of God, it takes on a comparative sense. Other nations worshiped numerous gods. Customarily, these gods were fashioned as idols. An idol can't move, speak, or hear. It can't respond to any situation. An idol just sits in its place. However, the living God speaks and listens. He acts. He isn't dead stone, metal, or wood. He's alive! He's the only living God.

³Even a sparrow finds a home, and a swallow, a nest for herself where she places her young—near your altars, LORD of Armies, my King and my God.

The courtyard of the temple was open, and the structure itself was bursting with ledges and crannies. Birds nested on its eaves and raised their young. The psalmist envied the birds because they dwelt in the temple. The altar represented the site where worshipers offered their sacrifices to God. Near this spot, God gave homes to His lesser creatures. Jesus used a similar illustration to teach His followers not to grow anxious about their physical needs (see Matt. 6:25-34).

Note the personal pronoun *my*. Worship begins in a personal relationship with God, a relationship in which the individual freely submits to God's authority.

⁴How happy are those who reside in your house, who praise you continually.

Happy denotes an optimal life that results from choosing to obey God. In some Bible translations it's rendered *blessed*. The verse points to two components of being happy. The first was attendance at the temple. According to the New Testament, the temple in Jerusalem has been replaced by a new reality. The Holy Spirit now makes His abode in believers (see John 14:27; 1 Cor. 6:19).

The second component of happiness is the choice to praise God continually. Jesus is the ultimate fulfillment of the symbolism portrayed in the Old Testament by the temple and the ark of the covenant. While the ark stood for the presence of God in the midst of His people, John 1:14 declares that "the Word," Jesus, "became flesh and dwelt among us," the presence of God in the midst of His people.

What role does passion play in worship? How does the expectation of God's presence affect that passion?

THE PRIORITY (Psalm 84:5-7)

⁵Happy are the people whose strength is in you, whose hearts are set on pilgrimage. ⁶As they pass through the Valley of Baca, they make it a source of spring water; even the autumn rain will cover it with blessings. ⁷They go from strength to strength; each appears before God in Zion.

Happy is the same word used in verse 4. The psalmist continued to describe the choices that produced an optimal life. The term *strength* denotes God protection of His people, finding security in God rather than in one's own assets.

The psalmist recognized the value of making a pilgrimage to the temple but characterized the trip as having difficulties and hardships. The Valley of Baca wasn't a specific geographical location. The name either means "valley of weeping" or "valley of desolation." It serves as an idiom for *sorrow*. God turns the pilgrim's dry places into an oasis.

This blessing is compared to the early rains that came in October and November. Western winds brought moisture off the Mediterranean Sea and dropped it on Palestine. In a region that averages only 25 inches of rain annually, the arrival of these rains brought joy and relief to its agrarian inhabitants.

The statement "They go from strength to strength" (v. 7) indicates that the lengthy journey didn't weaken pilgrims. Instead, they grew stronger as they moved closer to their destination. The anticipation of appearing before God in Zion invigorated them. Zion was originally the name given to the hill on which Jerusalem stood. In the Book of Psalms it most often denotes the temple built by Solomon. Later, it also came to refer to the heavenly Jerusalem, the site where the Messiah will appear at the end of time.

KEY DOCTRINE
The Kingdom of God

The Kingdom is the realm of salvation into which people enter by trustful, childlike commitment to Jesus Christ. Christians ought to pray and to labor that the Kingdom may come and God's will be done on earth.

What was the value of God's presence for the psalmist?
How does God's presence serve as a source of strength?

THE PRAYER (Psalm 84:8-9)

⁸LORD God of Armies, hear my prayer; listen, God of Jacob.
⁹Consider our shield, God; look on the face of your anointed one.

This verse presents two essential truths about prayer. First, though the psalmist was still a great distance away from the place where God had promised to hear Israel's prayers (see 1 Kings 8:29,38-39), the LORD God of Armies was sovereign over all creation. Therefore, He could hear His people wherever they might pray.

The second truth comes from the designation "God of Jacob" (v. 8). Jacob was the patriarch whose descendants formed the nation of Israel. The name Jacob means "he cheats." Jacob deceived his blind father and cheated his older brother out of his inheritance. God's choice of Jacob over Esau reminds us of God's grace. Neither Jacob nor Esau deserved God's favor. Likewise, God hears His people's prayers, not because they merit His ear but because of His grace.

The psalmist called on God to look with favor on the king, the annointed one whom he called "our shield" (v. 9). Israel's king was responsible for the protection of God's people. Annointing signified that God's power was present to enable them to carry out the duties of the office.

Why was it so important for the psalmist to ask God to direct the king? How did the realization that God anoints rulers and leaders influence the way the psalmist prayed?

THE PRESENCE (Psalm 84:10-12)

¹⁰Better a day in your courts than a thousand anywhere else.
I would rather stand at the threshold of the house of my God
than live in the tents of wicked people.

BIBLE SKILL

Dig deeper into the background and usage of key words or phrases.

Use a concordance to find other uses of the term *anointed* in the Bible. Read selected passages and make notes of findings that help you better understand the term. Read the entry for the term in a trusted Bible dictionary, adding to your notes. What key insights did you gain about the term?

The psalmist declared the joy of being in God's presence. The phrase "I would rather" signifies that this was a choice. Keep in mind this psalm is designated "a psalm of the sons of Korah." As previously noted, the sons of Korah were doorkeepers in the temple (see 1 Chron. 9:17-24; 26:1-19), an uncomfortable job. It required being on one's feet and possibly exposed to cold and rain. Still, the psalmist preferred serving at the door of the temple. Clearly, he loved the place of worship. Nothing on earth could compare to a moment near God.

¹¹For the LORD God is a sun and shield. The LORD grants favor and honor; he does not withhold the good from those who live with integrity. ¹²Happy is the person who trusts in you, LORD of Armies!

The psalmist called God "a sun and shield" (v. 11). As the light of our lives, God provides illumination and direction. As our shield, God provides protection. But God's goodness doesn't cease there. To those who trust in Him, God gives an optimal life.

One last time the psalmist addressed God as LORD of Armies. Here the title incorporates every attribute of God and summons people to either trust in Him or depend on something less. The person who decides to trust God will be happy, but anyone who doesn't trust God is doomed for destruction (see Ps. 1:4-6).

What modern illustration might convey the same trust in God that the psalmist expressed? What makes God's presence so compelling?

❯ OBEY THE TEXT

- Believers are to worship God passionately in light of who He is.

- God offers strength for life to those who seek to worship Him.

- Believers are to pray for their leaders and for God's direction as they lead.

- Believers are to respond to God's presence with worship and praise.

As a Bible-study group, share some of the blessings God has bestowed on you. Discuss how an awareness of these blessings affects the way you approach worship. Challenge one another to remember these blessings during your next worship experience.

List the names of leaders in your community, region, and country. Pray for God to direct their steps as they lead this week. Record your prayer below.

Evaluate your level of passion for being in God's presence. Look for things that diminish your passion. What actions do you need to take to increase your passion for being in God's presence?

MEMORIZE

Happy is the person who trusts in you,
LORD of Armies!—Psalm 84:12

USE THE SPACE PROVIDED TO MAKE OBSERVATIONS AND RECORD PRAYER
REQUESTS DURING THE GROUP EXPERIENCE FOR THIS SESSION.

MY THOUGHTS

Record insights and questions from the group experience.

_____

_____

_____

_____

_____

_____

MY RESPONSE

Note specific ways you'll put into practice the truth explored this week.

_____

_____

_____

_____

_____

_____

MY PRAYERS

List specific prayer needs and answers to remember this week.

_____

_____

_____

_____

_____

_____

_____

THE CREATOR

Believers should worship God above all else because He is sovereign.

UNDERSTAND THE CONTEXT

USE THE FOLLOWING PAGES TO PREPARE FOR YOUR GROUP TIME.

Psalm 95 may have been composed for the Festival of Booths. This week-long feast celebrated the ingathering of the harvest and commemorated Israel's exodus from Egyptian slavery. During this sacred holiday the Israelites erected temporary living quarters to remind them of God's providential care during the years when the nation wandered in the wilderness. Booths didn't signify privation and poverty but symbolized God's protection and preservation. Living in booths for a week reminded Israel of God's protection during a critical period in its history.

Psalm 95 combines a hymn of praise with a warning from God. The Festival of Booths was a joyful time. For six days the people lived in the fields and labored from sunrise to dark gathering the harvest. The agricultural principles that produced the crops were established by the Creator of heaven and earth (see Gen. 1:11-12,29-30), and He had given the Israelites the land where they farmed. Therefore, harvesting food called for praising God (see Deut. 8:7-10).

However, instead of rejoicing, the Israelites often complained. God answered the praise in verses 1-7a with a stern warning. He spoke directly to the worshipers, reminding them of His judgment against their faithless ancestors, the generation that perished during the 40 years in the wilderness. He mentioned only two examples but clearly implied they were symptomatic of a larger failure. God's warning wasn't confined to the Sinai covenant with Israel. It's equally applicable to Christians today. Verses 7b-11 are quoted and expounded on in Hebrews 3:7–4:13. God unmistakably warns that faithlessness to the gospel will incur an even worse fate than the one the Israelites suffered.

"A MAN CAN NO MORE DIMINISH GOD'S GLORY BY REFUSING TO WORSHIP HIM THAN A LUNATIC CAN PUT OUT THE SUN BY SCRIBBLING THE WORD 'DARKNESS' ON THE WALLS OF HIS CELL. BUT GOD WILLS OUR GOOD, AND OUR GOOD IS TO LOVE HIM … AND TO LOVE HIM WE MUST KNOW HIM: AND IF WE KNOW HIM, WE SHALL IN FACT FALL ON OUR FACES."—C. S. Lewis

➤ PSALM 95

Think About It

Highlight words and phrases that point to God's work in the world. What do these communicate about God's interaction with His creation?

Notice the change in voice that occurs in this psalm. What makes this change significant?

1 Come, let us shout joyfully to the LORD,
shout triumphantly to the rock of our salvation!
2 Let us enter his presence with thanksgiving;
let us shout triumphantly to him in song.
3 For the LORD is a great God,
a great King above all gods.
4 The depths of the earth are in his hand,
and the mountain peaks are his.
5 The sea is his; he made it.
His hands formed the dry land.
6 Come, let us worship and bow down;
let us kneel before the LORD our Maker.
7 For he is our God,
and we are the people of his pasture,
the sheep under his care.
Today, if you hear his voice:
8 Do not harden your hearts as at Meribah,
as on that day at Massah in the wilderness
9 where your fathers tested me;
they tried me, though they had seen what I did.
10 For forty years I was disgusted with that generation;
I said, "They are a people whose hearts go astray;
they do not know my ways."
11 So I swore in my anger,
"They will not enter my rest."

 Many psalms were intended to be sung. Go to the leader helps at *lifeway.com/explorethebible* to hear some of these psalms set to music and to download free worship arrangements of them.

EXPLORE THE TEXT

WHAT WORSHIP IS (Psalm 95:1-2)

¹**Come, let us shout joyfully to the LORD, shout triumphantly to the rock of our salvation!** ²**Let us enter his presence with thanksgiving; let us shout triumphantly to him in song.**

Just as highways are lined with signs that give us helpful instructions, the psalmist called for everyone to come and worship God. Two verbs convey the psalmist's exhortation. The first is "shout joyfully" (v. 1). The second verb is "shout triumphantly" (vv. 1-2). Together these verbs suggest noise similar to that in a sports arena when the home team scores. The people's exhilaration is directed toward the Lord. The Hebrew name Yahweh is used here, distinguishing the one true God from false deities.

"The rock of our salvation" (v. 1) is a metaphor that points to the security found in God as our Savior. God has shown Himself to be unchangeable and strong like a rock. The invitation to worship God in verse 2 also directs worshipers in how to enter God's presence, gratefully acknowledging that the central Person of worship is God.

Worship is a noun before it becomes a verb. Humans were created to worship God. A believer's state of being is to be made ready before the believer's physical expression of worship is exercised. This truth is seen in Amos 5:23, in which God rejected worship because the people's relationships with God and with one another were out of order. God said to take away the noise of their songs because those worshiping Him were

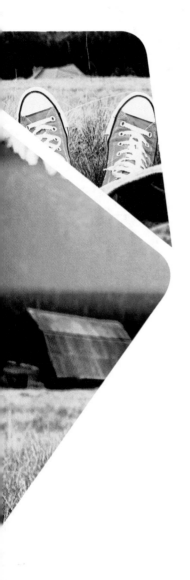

cheating the poor. Jesus also said some people worshiped Him with their lips, but their hearts were far from Him (see Matt. 15:8).

Based on Psalm 25:1-2, how would you define worship? What elements should be included in worship?

WHOM TO WORSHIP (Psalm 95:3-5)

³For the LORD is a great God, a great King above all gods.

The psalmist highlighted God as the great King, identifying Him by His covenant name, Yahweh (the LORD). This eliminated any false impression about who God is. Ancient Israel occupied a small geographic area. The surrounding neighbors venerated idols. This verse contrasted Yahweh with their pantheons of false deities. The adjective *great* asserted His superiority over all other gods. The portrayal of Yahweh as a great King proclaimed His sovereignty over these gods. The psalmist's comparison didn't imply that these gods were real. They weren't (see Isa. 44:6-20; 46:1-7). Rather, it simply acknowledged that pagans worshiped these alleged gods.

⁴The depths of the earth are in his hand, and the mountain peaks are his.

The depths of the earth and the mountain peaks represent two extremes on our planet. The first is hidden beneath the ground. The center of the earth is approximately 3,950 miles from the surface. The world's tallest mountain is Mount Everest, at 29,028 feet. Regardless of the numerical measurements of these two extremes, they're insignificant when compared to their Creator. They're in His hand. God firmly controls both.

⁵The sea is his; he made it. His hands formed the dry land.

Like "the depths of the earth" (v. 4), the sea represents a hidden mystery. Even today, with our modern research tools and techniques, the ocean hides unexplored secrets.

The Bible figuratively uses the hand of God as an idiom for His power and authority. God's power and authority over the sea were so absolute that when He spoke, the sea obeyed and yielded up dry land. Both sea and land belong to God because He created them.

In what ways does the earth point to the greatness of God as Creator? What parts of creation cause the greatest fear? How do these fearsome things point to God?

HOW TO WORSHIP (Psalm 95:6-7a)

⁶Come, let us worship and bow down; let us kneel before the LORD our Maker.

The psalmist directed all creation to approach God with humility and reverence, bowing before Him. An understanding of the respective roles in the relationship between God and humanity is essential to genuine worship. The Hebrew verb *worship* means "to prostrate oneself." It's the most common term for worship. The verb rendered "bow down" means "to fall to one's knees and bend the back in homage." Thus, the first verb conveys the spirit of worship; the second, a posture for worship. Bowing and kneeling are appropriate expressions of humility before God. Yet we must remember there are numerous other postures for worshiping God in Scripture. For example, lifting up the hands is a posture of supplication (see Ps. 28:2). Likewise, looking up can also be appropriate (see 123:1).

The verb *kneel*, which literally means "to bless," may suggest kneeling in order to receive a blessing. "Before the LORD" literally means "to the face of Yahweh." Yahweh is our Maker. This term incorporates the ideas that God is our Creator and He shapes our lives today.

⁷For he is our God, and we are the people of his pasture, the sheep under his care.

Humanity's role in the relationship can't be limited to servitude alone. To do so would defame God's nature. Elsewhere God defines His nature as love (see 1 John 4:8). Because love characterizes God, He cares for His covenant people. The relationship between God and Israel was comparable to that of a shepherd and his sheep. A shepherd protects his sheep from predators and other dangers. He ensures they have an adequate supply of fresh water and tender green grass.

He treats their injuries in order to restore their health. Our Creator didn't just create us; He actively works as our Shepherd. Everything we are or have must be attributed to God. Jesus asserted that He's the Good Shepherd (see John 10:7-18). In Him God provided for our ultimate spiritual well-being.

How is the image of a shepherd and his sheep a fitting metaphor for the relationship between God and His people?

WHEN TO WORSHIP (Psalm 95:7b-11)

⁷Today, if you hear his voice: …

Listening to God is a vital component of our relationship with Him. Jesus said the ideal shepherd called his sheep by name, and the sheep responded to his voice. At the same time, sheep never respond to strangers. Therefore, since Jesus is the Good Shepherd, if we're His sheep, we'll hear his voice. Obedience is implicit in hearing God's voice. The word *today* warns that responding to God is urgent. Obedience can't be postponed. Delay can cause serious harm.

How does God speak to His people? What are some impediments that keep His people from listening to Him?

⁸Do not harden your hearts as at Meribah, as on that day at Massah in the wilderness ⁹where your fathers tested me; they tried me, though they had seen what I did.

The psalmist warned readers about ignoring God, failing to teach about Him, and failing to worship Him. He pointed to past failures in Israel's history as illustrations. When God's people come before Him, they must be pliable so that He can shape them. "Harden your hearts" (v. 8) connotes being so stubborn that change is no longer possible.

On two occasions during Israel's wandering in the Sinai wilderness, the people rebelled against God and refused to trust Him to provide essential water. Both times God brought water from solid rock. One incident occurred shortly after the exodus from Egypt (see Ex. 17:1-7). The other occurred just before entering Canaan (see Num. 20:1-13). Between the two incidents God performed a multitude of miracles that demonstrated His care for Israel. Testing denotes proving the quality of something. Israel was commanded, "Do not test the LORD your God as you tested him at Massah" (Deut. 6:16). Nonetheless, the Israelites persisted in the opposite of worship—distrusting God even though they had seen the evidence of His power and provision.

¹⁰For forty years I was disgusted with that generation; I said, "They are a people whose hearts go astray; they do not know my ways."

The verb "I was disgusted" conveys a strong emotional loathing that causes the destruction of the object of the disgust. Thus, God expressed His total rejection of the generation Moses led out of Egypt. The people constantly made the wrong choices because they didn't know God's ways.

¹¹So I swore in my anger, "They will not enter my rest."

God holds people accountable for testing Him. Of the vast multitude that departed Egypt—there were six hundred thousand men of military age (see Ex. 12:37)—only two, Joshua and Caleb, entered Canaan. The rest died in the wilderness. Here entering His rest refers to enjoying the fullness of God's blessing (see Heb. 4:1-13). This comes from worshiping God continuously, both individually and corporately.

What are the dangers of failing to worship God? How does obedience affect worship? How are obedience and worship similar, and how are they different?

❯ OBEY THE TEXT

- All creation should celebrate its Creator.

- God should be worshiped as our Creator.

- All people should approach worship of the Creator with humility and reverence.

- Believers must consistently worship God, corporately and privately.

List ways to celebrate and worship God as Creator. What do you need to incorporate into your private worship practices? What do you need to incorporate into your public worship practices? Describe how you will do so.

Examine your attitude toward worship. How would you rate your humility and reverence when it comes to worship? What actions can you take to foster humility and reverence in your worship practices?

Discuss as a group ways of holding one another accountable for actively worshiping God. How can the group encourage private worship? What actions should the group take to encourage corporate worship?

MEMORIZE

Come, let us worship and bow down;
let us kneel before the LORD our Maker.
—Psalm 95:6

USE THE SPACE PROVIDED TO MAKE OBSERVATIONS AND RECORD PRAYER
REQUESTS DURING THE GROUP EXPERIENCE FOR THIS SESSION.

MY THOUGHTS

Record insights and questions from the group experience.

_____
_____
_____
_____
_____
_____

MY RESPONSE

Note specific ways you'll put into practice the truth explored this week.

_____
_____
_____
_____
_____
_____

MY PRAYERS

List specific prayer needs and answers to remember this week.

_____
_____
_____
_____
_____
_____

THE CONFESSION

The realization of sin should move us to confession and repentance.

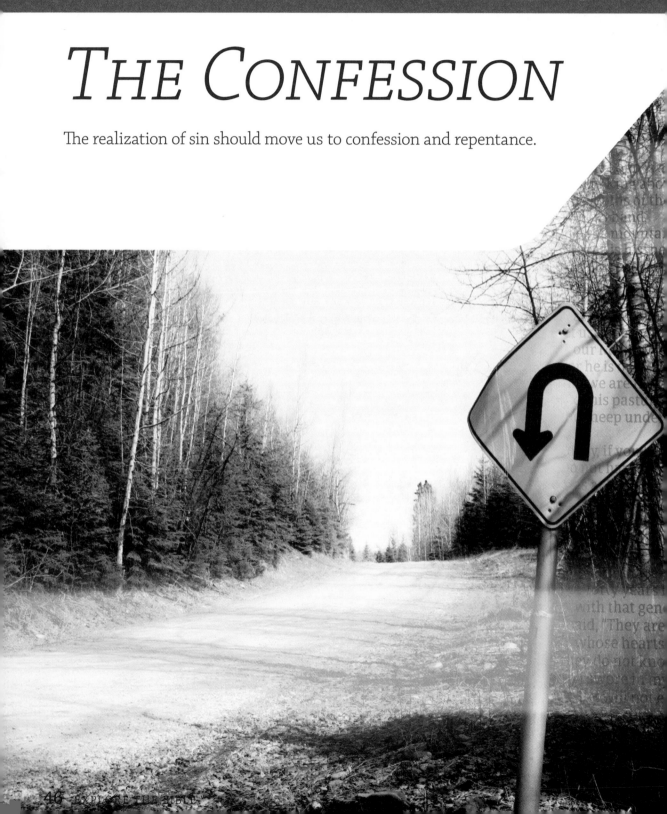

❯ UNDERSTAND THE CONTEXT

USE THE FOLLOWING PAGES TO PREPARE FOR YOUR GROUP TIME.

In Psalm 51 David petitioned God's forgiveness and reconciliation. This psalm provides detailed insight into David's repentance after Nathan confronted David with the sins of adultery and murder (see 2 Sam. 12:1-15). Using a story similar in proportion to David versus Goliath (see 1 Sam. 17), Nathan told David of a large ranch owner who stole and consumed the only lamb of a much smaller rancher. Outraged, David promised swift retribution for the callous rancher. Nathan then revealed the hard-hearted man in the story to be David since he had stolen another man's wife (Bathsheba) and covered his theft by having her husband (Uriah) killed in battle.

Our modern culture glamorizes sinful lifestyles. David's transparency in Psalm 51 reveals that sin breeds rebellion (see v. 1), guilt (see v. 2), shame (see vv. 3-4), disappointment (see v. 6), condemnation (see v. 7), and heartache (see v. 8). The good news of this psalm is that God's forgiveness can create a right heart (see v. 10), restored fellowship (see v. 11), renewed joy (see v. 12), a rejuvenated yearning for service (see vv. 12-13), and a responsive desire for worship (see vv. 14-17). If your life has veered off course, come before the Lord in honesty (see vv. 1-4), humility (see vv. 7-12), and a hunger for God (see vv. 14-17), as David did. Whether confronted or convicted, immediately confess and repent of all sin.

Sometimes forgiven believers wrestle with feelings of shame. Guilt (what we've done) must be distinguished from shame (who we are). Guilt is the normal response of a sinner to his or her sin. However, a forgiven sinner should no longer live in shame, because there's no condemnation in Christ (see Rom. 8:1). Jesus became sin so that we could become the righteousness of God (see 2 Cor. 5:21).

> "MANY MOURN FOR THEIR SINS, WHO DO NOT TRULY REPENT OF THEM; WEEP BITTERLY FOR THEM, YET CONTINUE IN LOVE AND IN LEAGUE WITH THEM."
> —*Matthew Henry*

How often am I repenting vs how often I am sitting in remorse?

➤ PSALM 51:1-17

Think About It

Circle words and phrases that point to feelings of remorse. How did these feelings affect David's confession?

Notice the ways David described the acts that led to his confession. What do these words or phrases reveal about the nature of sin?

1 Be gracious to me, God, according to your faithful love; according to your abundant compassion, blot out my rebellion.
2 Completely wash away my guilt and cleanse me from my sin.
3 For I am conscious of my rebellion, and my sin is always before me.
4 Against you—you alone—I have sinned and done this evil in your sight. So you are right when you pass sentence; you are blameless when you judge.
5 Indeed, I was guilty when I was born; I was sinful when my mother conceived me.
6 Surely you desire integrity in the inner self, and you teach me wisdom deep within.
7 Purify me with hyssop, and I will be clean; wash me, and I will be whiter than snow.
8 Let me hear joy and gladness; let the bones you have crushed rejoice.
9 Turn your face away from my sins and blot out all my guilt.
10 God, create a clean heart for me and renew a steadfast spirit within me.
11 Do not banish me from your presence or take your Holy Spirit from me.

Realignment

12 Restore the joy of your salvation to me, and sustain me by giving me a willing spirit.
13 Then I will teach the rebellious your ways, and sinners will return to you.
14 Save me from the guilt of bloodshed, God—God of my salvation—and my tongue will sing of your righteousness.
15 Lord, open my lips, and my mouth will declare your praise.
16 You do not want a sacrifice, or I would give it; you are not pleased with a burnt offering.
17 The sacrifice pleasing to God is a broken spirit. You will not despise a broken and humbled heart, God.

Many psalms were intended to be sung. Go to the leader helps at *lifeway.com/explorethebible* to hear some of these psalms set to music and to download free worship arrangements of them.

› EXPLORE THE TEXT

GUILTY AS CHARGED (Psalm 51:1-5)

¹Be gracious to me, God, according to your faithful love; according to your abundant compassion, blot out my rebellion.

Once David gave in to the sin of adultery, other sins followed. When he learned Bathsheba was pregnant with his child (see 2 Sam. 11:1-5), he ordered Uriah home from battle, hoping Uriah would spend the night with his wife. Being a man of integrity, Uriah refused the comforts of home while his men were in battle (see vv. 6-13). In desperation David had Uriah killed (see vv. 14-17). After allowing Bathsheba a period of mourning, David brought her into his palace as his wife under the guise of providing for the widow of a war hero (see vv. 26-27).

Sin didn't gratify David; instead, it led him on a downward spiral of deceit and death. David likely thought he had sufficiently covered his tracks and gotten away with his sin until God's messenger arrived about nine months later (see 2 Sam. 12:1-13).

Convicted, David realized his sin was an act of rebellion against God. He had broken the Sixth and Seventh Commandments by committing adultery and murder (see Ex. 20:13-14). As the king of Israel, David understood the severity of rebellion. His only recourse was to admit his guilt and seek God's mercy.

Because God is gracious and shows faithful love and abundant compassion, we too can turn to Him when we fall for sin's temptations. No matter the mess we make of our lives, God can rescue us as long as we take responsibility for our sin by admitting our guilt.

²Completely wash away my guilt and cleanse me from my sin. ³For I am conscious of my rebellion, and my sin is always before me. ⁴Against you—you alone—I have sinned and done this evil in your sight. So you are right when you pass sentence; you are blameless when you judge. ⁵Indeed, I was guilty when I was born; I was sinful when my mother conceived me.

David was riddled with guilt for destroying a marriage, killing an innocent man, and causing the death of his child (see 2 Sam. 12:14). His sin made him feel dirty inside. What dirt does to the body, sin does to the inner person. David needed cleansing that only God could provide. He was consumed with his wrongdoing. Every sinful word and every sinful act must have replayed over and over in his mind. No matter where he went or what he did, he couldn't escape his sin. He was ashamed before God and knew God was right to judge him. Do these sound like the words of someone who was enjoying life? No, these are the words of someone who experienced sin's heartache.

Notice the progression of David's confession. First, the rebellious sinner pleaded for God's grace, love, and compassion (see Psalm 51:1). Second, David begged for God's cleansing forgiveness (see v. 2). Third, the repentant king honestly admitted he had sinned (see v. 3). Fourth, David acknowledged that God, the true Judge, held him accountable for his wickedness (see v. 4). Fifth, he made no excuses for his unacceptable behavior (see v. 5). "Sinful when my mother conceived me" meant there had never been a time when he hadn't been a sinner. He had been born with sinful inclinations. David didn't hide, justify, or deny his sin. He admitted he was guilty as charged. Like David, we have committed sin and are just as guilty before God.

What are some ways people minimize or rationalize sin to deal with their guilt? Why is it easier to point out other people's sins than to acknowledge our own?

A PLEA FOR CLEANSING *(Psalm 51:6-13)*

⁶Surely you desire integrity in the inner self, and you teach me wisdom deep within.

Integrity comes from a Hebrew word meaning "stability, truth, and trustworthiness." David lost these virtues when he dove into sin. His life became unstable when he forsook God's truth, and as a result, he knew God could no longer trust him. David longed for a right relationship with God and with God's Word. He wanted God's wisdom to fill his heart and guide his life. He found himself in a desolate pit with the deep waters of sin drowning him, and he wanted out. David teaches us that the way back from sin starts with the desire to be whole again, recognizing the consequences of sin and craving God's forgiveness. Sin leads away from God, while spiritual wellness begins when we draw near to God (see Jas. 4:8), thirsting for Him above all else (see Ps. 40:1-2).

⁷Purify me with hyssop, and I will be clean; wash me, and I will be whiter than snow. ⁸Let me hear joy and gladness; let the bones you have crushed rejoice. ⁹Turn your face away from my sins and blot out all my guilt.

David asked God for two things: forgiveness and a changed life. Although the word *forgive* doesn't appear in the psalm, the psalmist made it clear that it was exactly what he needed from God. David pleaded with God: "Purify me with hyssop" (v. 7). Hyssop was a shrub with hairy stems. The priests used hyssop for sprinkling blood on sacrifices or water on people who needed ceremonial cleansing (see Lev. 14:4-6; Num. 19:18). Only by sprinkling with hyssop could a sinner be made holy and acceptable before God.

David also asked God to wash him. The cleaning David requested wasn't a physical bathing but a washing away of his sins. Only God could wash away the filth that had stained his heart, making him whiter than snow (see Isa. 1:18).

David asked God to replace his sorrow with gladness. God's conviction had crushed his bones, robbing him of joy. In such a sad state, he was unworthy of singing praises to God as he had done before (see 1 Chron. 13:8).

> **KEY DOCTRINE**
> *Salvation (Repentance)*
>
> Repentance is a genuine turning from sin toward God.

BIBLE SKILL

*Read, reflect on,
and emotionally
react to Bible verses.*

Focus on Psalm 51:1-2.
Read the verses aloud
several times, each time
emphasizing different
words or phrases. For
example, in one reading
emphasize each word
for *sin*. Then read the
verse again, emphasizing
all the verbs. Take
note of your thoughts
and feelings. What
feelings were evoked
by the different words
and phrases as you
emphasized them?

David begged God, "Turn your face away from my sins" (Ps. 51:9).
He knew God saw the mess he had made of his life (see Ps. 139:7).
Then David asked God, "Blot out all my guilt" (Ps. 51:9). The Hebrew
word for "blot out" is *maha*, meaning "to erase, abolish, destroy,
and utterly wipe away." David knew that he was a sinner and that
he needed what all sinners need: God's merciful forgiveness.

*What does a right relationship with God look like? What role
does forgiveness play in cultivating our relationship with God?*

¹⁰**God, create a clean heart for me and renew a steadfast spirit
within me. ¹¹Do not banish me from your presence or take your
Holy Spirit from me. ¹²Restore the joy of your salvation to me,
and sustain me by giving me a willing spirit. ¹³Then I will teach
the rebellious your ways, and sinners will return to you.**

David begged God to change his life. The word *create* translates
a Hebrew term that's used in the Old Testament only to refer to God's
creative work. David was asking for a change in his life that only God
could create. Sin had robbed David of intimacy with God. Sin had
caused David to feel alienated from God's presence and power.

David also asked God for the privilege of leading others back to God.
He would devote his life to helping other sinners find their way back
to the loving arms of God. In the remaining years of his life, David
wanted his life to bear fruit that honored God.

*How would you describe a forgiven heart? What actions
are required for a person to have a pure heart?*

DELIVERANCE THROUGH BROKENNESS
(Psalm 51:14-17)

¹⁴**Save me from the guilt of bloodshed, God—God of my
salvation—and my tongue will sing of your righteousness.
¹⁵Lord, open my lips, and my mouth will declare your praise.
¹⁶You do not want a sacrifice, or I would give it; you are not
pleased with a burnt offering. ¹⁷The sacrifice pleasing to God
is a broken spirit. You will not despise a broken and humbled
heart, God.**

Broken over his sin, David stopped doing things his way and started doing things God's way. In exchange for his murderous past (see v. 14), David gave three pieces of evidence of a repentant life. First, he offered God his unending praise. Because of his sins, David had lost the song God had placed in his heart. After David admitted his guilt and pleading for God's cleansing, his love for praising God returned.

Second, as the king, David was wealthy enough to offer God many sacrifices, but he knew God didn't want meaningless sacrifices or empty religious rituals. He longed for worship that pleased God.

Third, David offered God his brokenness. The repentant king offered God the only acceptable sacrifice: genuine repentance as evidenced by his broken spirit and humbled heart. The word *broken* in Hebrew is *shabar*, meaning "to break into pieces." David was broken over the pain his sin had caused him; those around him; and most of all, God.

Although God no longer requires sacrificial rituals, reconciliation with Him is more than just mouthing the right religious words. God doesn't look at our words; He looks at the condition of our hearts. His deliverance is reserved for those who are broken over their sinfulness and who desire to be right with Him. Approaching God with brokenness and humility over our sin is the first step toward deliverance from our guilt.

How are remorse and repentance related? How are they different? Can you have one without the other? Explain.

❯ OBEY THE TEXT

- Everyone has committed sin and, as a result, is guilty before God.

- Forgiveness of sin comes only through God's provision, His Son.

- Believers should approach God for forgiveness with brokenness and humility over their sin.

Discuss as a group how the fact that everyone is a sinner should affect your group. How can your group help restore people who have been broken by sin? With a spirit of biblical love and humility, consider appropriate ways of confrontation, reconciliation with God and the group, and accountability.

Record how you first became aware of your need for God's forgiveness. With whom can you share what you've written? As you share with that person, also share how you found forgiveness through His Son.

Spend time alone with God, asking Him to reveal to you sins that you need to confess to Him. Use Psalm 51 as a prayer, asking for forgiveness as God reveals sins to you.

MEMORIZE

God, create a clean heart for me and renew a steadfast spirit within me.—Psalm 51:10

USE THE SPACE PROVIDED TO MAKE OBSERVATIONS AND RECORD PRAYER
REQUESTS DURING THE GROUP EXPERIENCE FOR THIS SESSION.

MY THOUGHTS

Record insights and questions from the group experience.

_____

_____

_____

_____

_____

_____

MY RESPONSE

Note specific ways you'll put into practice the truth explored this week.

_____

_____

_____

_____

_____

_____

MY PRAYERS

List specific prayer needs and answers to remember this week.

_____

_____

_____

_____

_____

_____

THE LONGING

The hope of God's presence serves as encouragement during discouraging times.

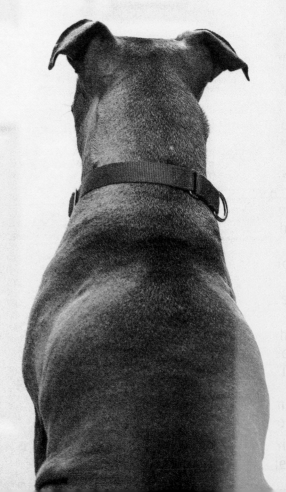

> UNDERSTAND THE CONTEXT

USE THE FOLLOWING PAGES TO PREPARE FOR YOUR GROUP TIME.

Many Bible scholars believe Psalms 42 and 43 were composed as a single psalm. Psalm 42 consists of two stanzas with identical refrains in verses 5 and 11. Psalm 43 has the same refrain in its final verse, so it appears to be a third stanza of Psalm 42.

Although the writer of this psalm isn't specifically identified, the superscription indicates it was written by the sons of Korah. The sons of Korah were Levites who were descendants of Kohath, the father of Korah (see 1 Chron. 6:22-48; 9:17-32; 2 Chron. 20:19). They produced and performed music while the tabernacle was in the wilderness and after the construction of the temple in Jerusalem. Eleven psalms are attributed to the sons of Korah (see Pss. 42; 44–49; 84–85; 87–88).

The writer of Psalm 42 found himself in exile, separated from God's people (see vv. 2-4), though the exact cause and place of his exile are unknown. With the privilege of serving as a Levite taken away from him, the writer fell into the deep crevice of despair (see vv. 5-6).

In spite of his suffering, the psalmist still praised the Lord, knowing God was his only hope (see vv. 5,8,11). He put his hope in God and continued praising the Lord.

In Psalm 42 we can see glimpses and hear echoes of Jesus, the Suffering Servant. Just as the psalmist shed tears (see v. 3), Jesus shed tears at Lazarus's tomb (see John 11:35) and wept over Jerusalem (see Luke 19:41). Compare the forsakenness experienced by the psalmist (see Ps. 42:9; 43:2) with the cry of dereliction or forsakenness voiced by Jesus on the cross in Mark 15:34. The presence of thirst (see Ps. 42:1-2) sounds familiar to the thirst Jesus felt for God the Father when He was on the cross (see John 19:28). Jesus can be trusted since He knows the pain of this life as well.

"OUR VISION IS SO LIMITED WE CAN HARDLY IMAGINE A LOVE THAT DOES NOT SHOW ITSELF IN PROTECTION FROM SUFFERING. THE LOVE OF GOD IS OF A DIFFERENT NATURE ALTOGETHER. IT DOES NOT HATE TRAGEDY. IT NEVER DENIES REALITY. … THE LOVE OF GOD DID NOT PROTECT HIS OWN SON. THAT WAS THE PROOF OF HIS LOVE."

—*Elisabeth Elliot*

› PSALM 42

Think About It

Notice the repetition of words and phrases that reveal the psalmist's emotional state. What does the repetition of these words and phrases reveal about the pain the psalmist was enduring?

1 As a deer longs for flowing streams, so I long for you, God.

2 I thirst for God, the living God. When can I come and appear before God?

3 My tears have been my food day and night, while all day long people say to me, "Where is your God?"

4 I remember this as I pour out my heart: how I walked with many, leading the festive procession to the house of God, with joyful and thankful shouts.

5 Why, my soul, are you so dejected? Why are you in such turmoil? Put your hope in God, for I will still praise him, my Savior and my God.

6 I am deeply depressed; therefore I remember you from the land of Jordan and the peaks of Hermon, from Mount Mizar.

7 Deep calls to deep in the roar of your waterfalls; all your breakers and your billows have swept over me.

8 The LORD will send his faithful love by day; his song will be with me in the night—a prayer to the God of my life.

9 I will say to God, my rock, "Why have you forgotten me? Why must I go about in sorrow because of the enemy's oppression?"

10 My adversaries taunt me, as if crushing my bones, while all day long they say to me, "Where is your God?"

11 Why, my soul, are you so dejected? Why are you in such turmoil? Put your hope in God, for I will still praise him, my Savior and my God.

 Many psalms were intended to be sung. Go to the leader helps at *lifeway.com/explorethebible* to hear some of these psalms set to music and to download free worship arrangements of them.

❯ EXPLORE THE TEXT

THIRSTY *(Psalm 42:1-4)*

¹As a deer longs for flowing streams, so I long for you, God. ²I thirst for God, the living God. When can I come and appear before God? ³My tears have been my food day and night, while all day long people say to me, "Where is your God?" ⁴I remember this as I pour out my heart: how I walked with many, leading the festive procession to the house of God, with joyful and thankful shouts.

A drought is a prolonged period of abnormally low rainfall. A four-year drought caused the Dust Bowl of the 1930s, leaving 2.5 million Americans homeless due to destructive dust clouds. Spiritual drought, like a drought of rain, can be just as hazardous, creating a lifeless existence even for God's people, a life void of joy and hope. Remembering the days when he had joyfully worshiped with others at God's house, the psalmist agonized over his spiritual dryness. He knew God alone could satisfy his spiritual thirst for His presence in the same way only cool water from flowing streams can quench a deer's physical thirst.

Taunting him, his critics constantly asked, "Where is your God?" (v. 3). With their cruel question they implied God had deserted the psalmist, which only added to his grief. Though reasons for spiritual dryness are numerous, the results are the same: feelings of isolation from God, unasked prayers, apathy toward Bible study, a lack of desire for worship, and lost contact with fellow believers.

This spiritual wasteland isn't a location but a condition of the heart. No one is immune from the disease of spiritual drought, no matter how long he or she has been a Christian. As this psalmist struggled with the feeling of spiritual drought, he remembered a better day. He recalled a time when he led a festive procession to the temple that included many others who followed him. There in the house of God they worshiped with joy and thanksgiving.

These verses provide two clues to overcoming spiritual dryness. First, the psalmist recognized his spiritual need. Verse 1 is an honest confession of his current relationship with God. He no longer felt close to God. An honest evaluation is the first step toward wellness.

Second, the psalmist thirsted for God. A deer pants for a reason. Perhaps it has been chased by a predator or can't find water. Water is essential, not optional. Whenever we feel separated from the Lord, we must make seeking Him our highest priority. Believers must pay attention to their spiritual lives or else see it shrivel.

What does a thirst for God look like? How can believers create a thirst for God?

DROWNING *(Psalm 42:5-8)*

⁵Why, my soul, are you so dejected? Why are you in such turmoil? Put your hope in God, for I will still praise him, my Savior and my God. ⁶I am deeply depressed; therefore I remember you from the land of Jordan and the peaks of Hermon, from Mount Mizar. ⁷Deep calls to deep in the roar of your waterfalls; all your breakers and your billows have swept over me. ⁸The LORD will send his faithful love by day; his song will be with me in the night—a prayer to the God of my life.

In his despair the psalmist's mood took a radical turn from drought to a raging storm inside him. His inner turmoil was more than he could stand. The waves of deep despair rolled over him as if he had fallen off a capsized boat in the middle of the ocean.

The psalmist felt abandoned by God, and the futility of his situation consumed him. He had to take action. First, he put his hope in God.

Many people have hope, but the object of their hope is misplaced. Only by placing our hope in God can we find the help needed to weather the storms of life. Job overcame his afflictions with godly hope (see Job 13:15). Jeremiah reminded the exiles that godly hope would help them return home (see Jer. 29:11). Paul taught that godly hope will never disappoint (see Rom. 5:4-5). Believers have a living hope, for our hope is in a living Savior (see 1 Pet. 1:3).

Second, the psalmist praised God. At first, with a broken spirit, such praise can seem awkward or forced, but God is worthy of praise even when we don't feel like worshiping. Though worship may not remove the dark clouds from your life, it opens the doors of your heart and spirit, giving God an avenue for His healing touch. Notice the psalmist called God his Savior. Even though the psalmist couldn't return to the temple, he declared God was his Savior nevertheless.

Third, the psalmist remembered God. He promised to remember Him from the land of Jordan and the peaks of Hermon and from Mount Mizar. The exact location of Mount Mizar isn't known, though the name means "little mountain." Mount Hermon, at some 9,100 feet, is the highest mountain in the region, and it has three peaks. The psalmist might have been living in exile there. The region is approximately 125 miles from Jerusalem, but it might as well have been a million miles, given his desire to worship at the temple and his inability to do so.

Pain has many unintended side effects, one of which is forgetfulness. In the storms of life, believers often forget what God has done for them. Instead of being grateful, they narrowly focus their gaze on their current situation. By remembering who God is and what He has done for us, we can see the light at the end of the tunnel—maybe faintly at first but a light nonetheless.

Finally, the psalmist prayed to God. When we're in misery, we often turn inward to protect ourselves from further harm. When we do, we often stop doing the very thing that will help us cope with our situation—prayer. Much like praise, praying may seem useless at first because of the condition of our hearts. When we start, our prayers may seem more like an inquisition as we question God. When we finish praying, we must spend time listening to God and His words. Like the psalmist, we must ask for God's sustaining faithful love

KEY DOCTRINE
God the Holy Spirit

The Holy Spirit cultivates Christian character, comforts believers, and seals believers for the day of final redemption. His presence in Christians guarantees that God will bring them into the fullness of the stature of Christ.

for both our days and nights. In verse 8 the psalmist used the name LORD (Yahweh), meaning the self-existent and eternal God. The psalmist reminds us that when we pray, our prayers reach the throne of the God of heaven. Even when we can't see God's face, we can trust His heart, knowing that He cares (see 1 Pet. 5:7).

How can unresolved despair produce more despair? What role should a person's faith play in facing a situation that could cause despair in life?

CRUSHED *(Psalm 42:9-11)*

⁹**I will say to God, my rock, "Why have you forgotten me? Why must I go about in sorrow because of the enemy's oppression?"** ¹⁰**My adversaries taunt me, as if crushing my bones, while all day long they say to me, "Where is your God?"** ¹¹**Why, my soul, are you so dejected? Why are you in such turmoil? Put your hope in God, for I will still praise him, my Savior and my God.**

This psalmist raised questions about why God had forgotten him, why he must go about in sorrow because of the enemy's oppression. Often people in dire circumstances feel abandoned by God. The psalmist relayed those feelings in verse 9. Yet no matter how deeply believers feel abandoned by God, the depths of our feelings don't reflect the true reality. God has promised never to desert His people (see Isa. 49:15; Heb. 13:5).

The psalmist went from being thirsty in a spiritual drought (see Ps. 42:1-4) to being drowned in a spiritual storm (see vv. 5-8) to being crushed by words of accusation (see vv. 9-11). Notice what the psalmist called his oppressors: enemies and adversaries. They taunted him and his God. They delighted in repeatedly causing him pain. They were adversarial, confrontational, and mean-spirited.

Let's be honest: words hurt. They cut deep, leaving emotional, relational, and spiritual scars, driving us deeper into despair. How did the adversaries' words make this psalmist feel? He was full of *sorrow*, a word that means "to mourn in a blackened sackcloth." This word expressed a deep emotion that moved beyond mourning. Without any sign of relief, he felt as if his bones were crushing under the weight of their condemnation. He felt helpless as people attacked his faith with questions about the power of his God. As a result, the psalmist fell deeper into despair and turmoil.

While weaker men might have succumbed to the intense persecution, the psalmist cried out to God. He pleaded for God's help and reassurance that He was with him (see Ps. 23:4). He looked for God's help to shield his soul from the piercing words of his aggressors. He once again reaffirmed that his hope and praise were in his Savior and his God. He declared his allegiance to God even in times when opposition taunted him and questioned the power of God.

Though our attacks may not be as severe as what the psalmist experienced, they are real nonetheless. Menacing opposition, malicious comments, and character assassination are tools of Satan. Unfortunately, the devil sometimes delivers hurtful words through family, friends, and even other believers. When we feel crushed by the devil's blows, we must first seek God as our fortress and tell Him our hurts. God's presence serves as encouragement during discouraging times. Then we must trust Him for deliverance, remembering that one day our deliverance will be complete when the Lamb leads us to springs of living water (see Rev. 7:17).

How does the promise of God's presence serve as encouragement during hurtful times? How does His faithful presence function as proof of His future promises?

❯ OBEY THE TEXT

- Believers should pay attention to their spiritual lives and cultivate a longing to spend time with God.

- God is always present, even in the most difficult circumstances.

- Believers can praise God even when they face difficulties and uncertainties.

Review your regular habits, especially your habit of spending time with God. What time of day is best for you? How can you schedule a daily time with God that won't get pushed aside by other obligations? What can you do to protect your daily time with God?

Ask others in your group to describe times when they were aware of God's presence while facing a difficult situation. Record insights gained from their stories. Discuss ways the group can represent God to others who are facing difficulties.

Create a list of reasons you have for praising God. Include the challenges that lie before you. Take time to thank God for what He has done and what He will do as He walks with you through these challenges.

MEMORIZE

The LORD will send his faithful love by day;
his song will be with me in the night—
a prayer to the God of my life.—Psalm 42:8

MY THOUGHTS

Record insights and questions from the group experience.

MY RESPONSE

Note specific ways you'll put into practice the truth explored this week.

MY PRAYERS

List specific prayer needs and answers to remember this week.

❯ GETTING STARTED

OPENING OPTIONS: Choose one of the following to open the group discussion.

WEEKLY QUOTATION DISCUSSION STARTER: "When men are living in sin, they go from bad to worse. At first they merely *walk* in the counsel of the careless and ungodly, who forget God … but after that, they become habituated to evil, and they *stand* in the way of open sinners who willfully violate God's commandments."—Charles H. Spurgeon

> ❯ What's your initial response to this week's quotation?

> ❯ What are striking distinctions between those who live in sin and those who seek righteousness?

> ❯ Today we'll look at two paths: the path of life and the path of death. We'll see that both paths are available to us. The former is a gift that God, in His grace, has put at our fingertips. The latter is an avoidable tragedy that, regrettably, many people choose for themselves.

CREATIVE ACTIVITY: Before the group meets, print enough copies of Robert Frost's poem "The Road Not Taken" for everyone to have one. When the group arrives, ask a volunteer to read the poem aloud. Then use the following questions to begin discussion.

> ❯ What's the message of this poem? Why do you think this poem is adored and well known?

> ❯ Have you ever looked back at a specific time in your life and wondered what would have happened if you had chosen a different path or made a different decision? If participants are willing, ask a few of them to share examples.

> ❯ Explain that in this poem Frost described the tension of not being able to travel two paths simultaneously and discover where each one leads. Explain that we have two paths to choose from—the path of life and the path of death—and Scripture tells us where each path leads.

❯ UNDERSTAND THE CONTEXT

PROVIDE BACKGROUND: Briefly introduce members to Psalms, pointing out the major themes and any information that will help them understand Psalm 1 (see pp. 7 and 9). Then, to help people personally connect today's context with the original context, use the following questions and statements.

> ❯ The Book of Psalms opens by exploring the tension between living in sin and seeking righteousness. Although the author of Psalm 1 isn't known for certain, let's consider for a moment King David, the most prolific author in the Book of Psalms. What do we know about David's personal struggles with this tension between living in sin and seeking righteousness?

> ❯ As we'll see in today's passage, happiness is given to the righteous but remains ever elusive for the wicked. When we say "happiness," we're referring to blessedness, a sense of joy and contentment that comes only from the Lord. How do people pursue happiness today? In what ways is our culture getting it right, and in what ways are we getting it wrong?

> Psalm 1 is a wisdom psalm, meaning it instructs us in living wisely versus living foolishly. Although sin tempts us with promises to fulfill us and make us happy, we'll see in today's passage that sin *always* leads to death. Righteousness, on the other hand, leads to life.

❯ EXPLORE THE TEXT

READ THE BIBLE: Ask a volunteer to read Psalm 1.

DISCUSS: Use the following questions to discuss group members' initial reactions to the text.

> What immediately stands out to you in this text as a theme or primary point? What do you find encouraging, timely, or convicting?

> In verse 1 the psalmist used the verbs *walk*, *stand*, and *sit*. What do these verbs communicate to us about the subtle progression and entrapment of sin?

> In verses 3-4 the righteous are compared to a tree and the wicked to chaff. What do these images communicate to us? How do you feel when you read about the judgment of the wicked?

> In what ways has obedience to God produced fruit in your life? Conversely, in what ways have you experienced the destructive progression of sin?

> What does Psalm 1 communicate to us about the day of judgment?

> What else does this text teach us about God? About ourselves?

> What other questions or observations do you have?

NOTE: Provide ample time for group members to share responses and questions about the text. Don't feel pressured to prioritize the printed agenda over group members' personal experiences. If time allows, discuss responses to the questions in the personal reading.

❯ OBEY THE TEXT

RESPOND: Foster an environment of openness and action. Help individuals apply biblical truth to specific areas of personal thought, attitude, and/or behavior.

> To follow and delight in the Lord's instruction, we must first know the Lord's instruction. What steps can you take to better know the Lord's instruction and therefore more fully delight in it?

> Think of people in your life who are currently on the path that leads to death. In what ways will today's message about coming judgment affect the way you share your faith with them?

PRAY: Close by expressing delight in the Lord and His instruction. Thank Him for sharing His wisdom and righteousness with us.

> ## GETTING STARTED

OPENING OPTIONS: Choose one of the following to open the group discussion.

WEEKLY QUOTATION DISCUSSION STARTER: "Never be afraid to trust an unknown future to a known God."—Corrie Ten Boom

> > What's your initial response to this week's quotation?

> > Why do you think people often have difficulty trusting God with the future? What else do you have difficulty trusting God with?

> > King David knew the stresses of an unknown future. As the king, he faced a variety of threats. He didn't know where the next attack against his kingdom would come from, and he wasn't certain what calamities might overtake his people. However, as we'll see in today's session, David trusted God as his Shepherd, believing He would meet his needs.

CREATIVE ACTIVITY: Before the group meets, visit YouTube and search "Do sheep obey only their master's voice?" Preview the top search results and find a video that shows a group of people unsuccessfully attempting to call sheep. You should find that when it's the shepherd's turn, all of the sheep come running at the sound of his voice. When everyone arrives, share the video and then use the following statements and questions to begin discussion.

> > Why do you think certain people failed to get the sheep's attention? Why do you think the sheep came when their shepherd called?

> > Do you think the sheep trusted their shepherd's call from day one, or did they learn to trust him over time? How do you suppose the shepherd earned their trust?

> > Shepherds earn the trust of their sheep by caring for their needs. They feed them, guide them across great distances, and protect them from various threats. Likewise, as we'll see in today's passage, God is our Shepherd, the One who cares for us as no one else can.

> ## UNDERSTAND THE CONTEXT

PROVIDE BACKGROUND: Briefly introduce members to major themes, information, and ideas that will help them understand Psalm 23 (see p. 17). Then, to help people personally connect today's context with the original context, use the following questions and statements.

> > Before becoming king, David was a shepherd. He knew firsthand the trust that sheep have in their shepherd. Before his life was over, David intimately understood what it meant to trust God as his Shepherd, giving every care and need to the Lord. He faced off against Goliath. Saul attempted to have him killed. His son Absalom plotted against his father before being killed in battle against David's army. Through it all David trusted God as his Shepherd.

> David leaned heavily on the Lord during his times of greatest need. Do you find it easier or more difficult to lean on God as your Shepherd when times are tough? Why?

> We'll see in today's passage that the time for trusting the Lord is now, whether we're peacefully resting beside life's quiet waters or walking through life's darkest valleys.

❯ EXPLORE THE TEXT

READ THE BIBLE: Ask a volunteer to read Psalm 23.

DISCUSS: Use the following questions to discuss group members' initial reactions to the text.

> What immediately stands out to you in this text as a theme or primary point? What do you find encouraging, timely, or convicting?

> David used the pronoun *my* when referring to God as his Shepherd. What are mental, emotional, or spiritual obstacles that prevent people from grasping that the Lord is their personal Shepherd?

> David gladly acknowledged his need for God as his Shepherd. Why do some people refuse to concede that they need a Shepherd? Why are people often determined to lead, protect, and provide for themselves?

> What are some ways God has revealed Himself as your Shepherd and provided for your daily needs?

> What else does this text teach us about God? About ourselves?

> What other questions or observations do you have?

NOTE: Provide ample time for group members to share responses and questions about the text. Don't feel pressured to prioritize the printed agenda over group members' personal experiences. If time allows, discuss responses to the questions in the personal reading.

❯ OBEY THE TEXT

RESPOND: Foster an environment of openness and action. Help individuals apply biblical truth to specific areas of personal thought, attitude, and/or behavior.

> David wrote Psalm 23 as a song of worship celebrating the Lord as our Shepherd. Similarly, what can you do to outwardly communicate to others your faith in the Lord as your Shepherd?

> Who in your life is currently walking through a dark valley? How can you use David's experiences and the message of Psalm 23 to encourage them to place their trust in the Lord?

PRAY: Close by asking each person to thank God for acting as their Shepherd in one specific way in his or her life.

❯ GETTING STARTED

OPENING OPTIONS: Choose one of the following to open the group discussion.

WEEKLY QUOTATION DISCUSSION STARTER: "I want the presence of God Himself, or I don't want anything at all to do with religion. You would never get me interested in the old maids' social club with a little bit of Christianity thrown in to give it respectability. I want all that God has, or I don't want any." —A. W. Tozer

> ❯ What's your initial response to this week's quotation?

> ❯ In what ways do Christians today sometimes distract themselves from God's presence, even in the context of church activities?

> ❯ In today's passage we'll see a heart completely fixated on the presence of the Lord. The psalmist's words will show us what it means to value nearness to God above all else.

CREATIVE ACTIVITY: Before the group meets, search online for clean, inoffensive "Would you rather … ?" questions. Ideally, these questions should cause participants to evaluate their preferences (for example, "Would you rather spend the next year in a small town with close friends or travel the world by yourself?"). When everyone arrives, use the following activity and questions to begin discussion.

> ❯ Read the "Would you rather … ?" questions you selected. After each question allow volunteers time to share their answers before moving on to the next question. Ask participants what made them select one option over the other.

> ❯ Some of these questions were trickier than others. What criterion did you use for choosing between the more difficult "Would you rather … ?" options?

> ❯ As we'll see in today's passage, the psalmist's primary concern was God's presence. He would rather be near God than enjoy any worldly comforts.

❯ UNDERSTAND THE CONTEXT

PROVIDE BACKGROUND: Briefly introduce members to major themes, information, and ideas that will help them understand Psalm 84 (see p. 27). Then, to help people personally connect today's context with the original context, use the following questions and statements.

> ❯ Psalm 84 is a psalm of the Korahites, who were gatekeepers in the temple. In his zeal the psalmist could have said, "I want to be a high priest! I want to enter holy of holies!" Instead, today's passage makes a case for the joy of God's presence, even as a gatekeeper. The psalmist would rather stand outside the temple at the gate than enjoy worldly comforts in the tents of the wicked.

> ❯ What kinds of problems arise today when people prioritize the comforts of the world over the security and pleasure of God's presence?

> The people of God long and yearn to enter the presence of the living God. We're drawn to His presence and then compelled by His presence to worship and praise Him.

❯ EXPLORE THE TEXT

READ THE BIBLE: Ask a volunteer to read Psalm 84.

DISCUSS: Use the following questions to discuss group members' initial reactions to the text.

> What immediately stands out to you in this text as a theme or primary point? What do you find encouraging, timely, or convicting?

> What are the different names the psalmist used to refer to God? What do these names tell us about God's attributes?

> According to the psalmist, what are sources of happiness in the lives of God's people? In what ways does God's presence give you joy and strength?

> In verse 4 the psalmist referred to the joy of worshiping God continually in the temple. What's the modern equivalent of God's temple for believers today? What do you think continual worship looks like for Christians today?

> The Valley of Baca in verse 6 is translated as "the valley of weeping." When was a time when God showed up in your valley of weeping and transformed it into a place of life and blessing?

> What else does this text teach us about God? About ourselves?

> What other questions or observations do you have?

NOTE: Provide ample time for group members to share responses and questions about the text. Don't feel pressured to prioritize the printed agenda over group members' personal experiences. If time allows, discuss responses to the questions in the personal reading.

❯ OBEY THE TEXT

RESPOND: Foster an environment of openness and action. Help individuals apply biblical truth to specific areas of personal thought, attitude, and/or behavior.

> What adjustments can you make this week to kindle a greater passion for God's presence?

> What are some things you've prioritized over God's presence and worship? How can you as a group encourage one another to faithfully seek God's presence and respond with worship?

PRAY: Spend time reflecting on moments when God's presence was clear and powerful. Thank God for being close, as well as for the strength and joy that accompany His presence.

❯ GETTING STARTED

OPENING OPTIONS: Choose one of the following to open the group discussion.

WEEKLY QUOTATION DISCUSSION STARTER: "A man can no more diminish God's glory by refusing to worship Him than a lunatic can put out the sun by scribbling the word 'darkness' on the walls of his cell. But God wills our good, and our good is to love Him. ... and to love Him we must know Him: and if we know Him, we shall in fact fall on our faces."—C. S. Lewis

> ❯ What's your initial response to this week's quotation?

> ❯ When was a time you withheld worship from God? What was the reason?

> ❯ What has been one of your greatest moments of worship? In what ways was this experience directly affected by a recognition of God as Creator?

> ❯ In today's passage we'll see that God, as our Creator, is always worthy of our worship.

CREATIVE ACTIVITY: Before the group meets, find a video clip of people meeting their idols. Or you may choose to share a time you met someone you follow and respect. When everyone arrives, share the video or story and then use the following question to begin discussion.

> ❯ Why do people react with so much emotion when they meet someone famous?

> ❯ At what point does fandom become idolatry and false worship?

> ❯ When people meet celebrities, they may cry, scream, or look stunned. Today we'll see that our proper response when we encounter God, our Creator, is to worship Him. He alone is worthy.

❯ UNDERSTAND THE CONTEXT

PROVIDE BACKGROUND: Briefly introduce members to major themes, information, and ideas that will help them understand Psalm 95 (see p. 37). Then, to help people personally connect today's context with the original context, use the following questions and statements.

> ❯ It's thought that Psalm 95 was written for the Festival of Booths, a feast commemorating Israel's exodus from Egypt. God's faithfulness to the Israelites during the exodus is a recurring subject in Israel's worship throughout Scripture. Like the Israelites, we all have memories we recall that prompt us to worship God. What specific memory of God's faithfulness in your life do you return to often? Why does this memory still compel you to celebrate God's work?

> ❯ Today's passage touches on God's faithfulness and His people's unfaithfulness. In what ways does God's faithfulness move us to worship? In what ways can recalling the past failures of God's people also move us to worship?

› We'll see that there's always a reason to worship God, and there are always consequences for withholding worship from Him. God alone gave us life, and He alone sustains our lives. Both facts point us to one conclusion: our Creator is worthy of our worship.

〉 EXPLORE THE TEXT

READ THE BIBLE: Ask a volunteer to read Psalm 95.

DISCUSS: Use the following questions to discuss group members' initial reactions to the text.

› What immediately stands out to you in this text as a theme or primary point? What do you find encouraging, timely, or convicting?

› Based on today's passage, what are a few different expressions of worship that we can incorporate into our worship?

› Do we have to be on our knees in order to worship God? What's the significance of kneeling in worship to God? What does the gesture reveal about our hearts?

› Some people believe God created everything but that He's no longer interested in our lives and daily affairs. In what ways does verse 7 counter this idea?

› How would you describe a hardened heart in your own words? How does a hardened heart interfere with our worship of God?

› What else does this text teach us about God? About ourselves?

› What other questions or observations do you have?

NOTE: Provide ample time for group members to share responses and questions about the text. Don't feel pressured to prioritize the printed agenda over group members' personal experiences. If time allows, discuss responses to the questions in the personal reading.

〉 OBEY THE TEXT

RESPOND: Foster an environment of openness and action. Help individuals apply biblical truth to specific areas of personal thought, attitude, and/or behavior.

› In what ways does God's creation inspire and inform our worship of God? How does reflecting on God's role as Creator affect our obedience to Him?

› What role does listening have in worship? How can increase our sensitivity to God's voice?

PRAY: Close by asking God to open the hearts of group members so that each person will hear His voice. Take time to thank Him for the gift of life.

› GETTING STARTED

OPENING OPTIONS: Choose one of the following to open the group discussion.

WEEKLY QUOTATION DISCUSSION STARTER: "Many mourn for their sins, who do not truly repent of them; weep bitterly for them, yet continue in love and in league with them."—Matthew Henry

> › What's your initial response to this week's quotation?

> › How does true repentance differ from simple remorse?

> › Today's Scripture passage shows that simple guilt over our sin is incomplete if it isn't accompanied by confession and repentance.

CREATIVE ACTIVITY: Before the group meets, think of a time when you or someone you know ignored a problem until it got worse (for example, you ignored a cavity and had to have a root canal, or you ignored the fact that your car was running hot, and the head gasket blew). When the group arrives, use the following questions to begin discussion.

> › Why would someone choose to ignore clear signs of trouble? What possible reasons could we have for putting off getting the help we need?

> › Is there ever a benefit in ignoring a problem? Why or why not?

> › Sin is a real problem that can't simply be ignored. Today we'll see a picture of confession and repentance, the only appropriate responses to the guilt of sin.

› UNDERSTAND THE CONTEXT

PROVIDE BACKGROUND: Briefly introduce members to major themes, information, and ideas that will help them understand Psalm 51:1-17 (see p. 47). Then, to help people personally connect today's context with the original context, use the following questions and statements.

> › David was acquainted with the guilt of sin, as we all are. Although remembered today as a man after God's own heart (see 1 Sam. 13:14), David infamously committed adultery with Bathsheba and had her husband, Uriah, killed in battle. Public opinion widely varies on the topic of sin, but the general cultural consensus seems to be that adultery and murder are wrong. Why does our society generally agree on the evil of adultery and murder?

> › The realization of his sin led David to repentance, which we glimpse in Psalm 51. Why can it be important for us to observe confession and repentance in others? Specifically, what can we learn from reading about David's contrition in today's passage?

> › Not everyone responds to guilt the same way. As the people of God, however, we ultimately share this in common: our guilt leads us to God's grace, which moves us to repentance.

❭ EXPLORE THE TEXT

READ THE BIBLE: Ask a volunteer to read Psalm 51:1-17.

DISCUSS: Use the following questions to discuss group members' initial reactions to the text.

> ❭ What immediately stands out to you in this text as a theme or primary point? What do you find encouraging, timely, or convicting?

> ❭ How many times in today's passage did David express remorse? How would the overall tone of this psalm change if it didn't also include David's repentance?

> ❭ In what ways are remorse and repentance similar? In what ways are they different?

> ❭ What role does repentance have in forgiveness? Can we hope to be free of our sins without first confessing our sins? Why or why not?

> ❭ In verses 16-17 David asserted that religious gestures, such as sacrifices, are insufficient substitutes for repentance; instead, God desires brokenness and humility, both of which inevitably accompany true repentance. In what ways do believers today attempt to take shortcuts to God's forgiveness without allowing themselves to experience their own brokenness?

> ❭ What else does this text teach us about God? About ourselves?

> ❭ What other questions or observations do you have?

NOTE: Provide ample time for group members to share responses and questions about the text. Don't feel pressured to prioritize the printed agenda over group members' personal experiences. If time allows, discuss responses to the questions in the personal reading.

❭ OBEY THE TEXT

RESPOND: Foster an environment of openness and action. Help individuals apply biblical truth to specific areas of personal thought, attitude, and/or behavior.

> ❭ How has God used your moments of greatest brokenness to create a pure heart in you? Discuss with the group ways you can use these experiences to encourage others in the midst of their brokenness.

> ❭ Is someone in your life relying on religious gestures for forgiveness? What about someone blatantly, unapologetically walking in sin? True repentance takes place when our very real sins are confronted by God's very real grace, and we're left broken and humble. What will you do to communicate God's forgiveness to others?

PRAY: Close by praying together the words of Psalm 51:1-17.

› GETTING STARTED

OPENING OPTIONS: Choose one of the following to open the group discussion.

WEEKLY QUOTATION DISCUSSION STARTER: "Our vision is so limited we can hardly imagine a love that does not show itself in protection from suffering. The love of God is of a different nature altogether. It does not hate tragedy. It never denies reality. ... The love of God did not protect His own Son. That was the proof of His love."—Elisabeth Elliot

> › What's your initial response to this week's quotation?

> › In what ways does Christ's suffering help us make sense of our own emotional, physical, or spiritual suffering? How can we draw strength from the suffering Christ endured?

> › In today's passage we'll glimpse the brokenness of a man who felt isolated from God. The psalmist's words show us the importance of maintaining hope in God and continuously seeking His presence, believing He will always bring us through the dark times when He seems distant.

CREATIVE ACTIVITY: When the group arrives, ask for a show of hands from those who follow celebrities on social media. If you have a Twitter account, pull out your phone and tweet at a celebrity (preferably a public figure who isn't controversial and has many followers). If not, ask a volunteer to pull out their phone and tweet at a celebrity. Then use the following statements and questions to begin discussion.

> › What would happen if we just sat here and waited until the celebrity tweeted us back? What are a few reasons this celebrity will likely never respond?

> › When we reach out to someone for help and they answer our call, what should our response be? When people are present and available in our times of need, what does this tell us about them?

> › In all likelihood we could tweet at celebrities all day and never get a response. They probably wouldn't even read our message. Every believer endures seasons of spiritual drought and darkness, times when it seems as if God can't hear us. God, however, is always ready to listen and is always poised to act on our behalf. As we'll see in today's passage, our hope is in God's presence at all times and in all circumstances.

› UNDERSTAND THE CONTEXT

PROVIDE BACKGROUND: Briefly introduce members to major themes, information, and ideas that will help them understand Psalm 42 (see p. 57). Then, to help people personally connect today's context with the original context, use the following questions and statements.

> › The early church sang psalms in their worship. How do you feel about worship songs that explore hard truths and dark seasons of life, such as Psalm 42? What's the value in incorporating these topics into our worship?

> In what ways do we see the tug-of-war between the moodiness of our emotions and the resilience of our faith in today's passage? If you were in the psalmist's shoes, what are a few adjectives you would use to describe the pain of feeling far from God?

> As we see in verse 11, faith and hope get the last word in today's passage. Why is this important?

> We'll see how our longing for God's presence is always ultimately satisfied; our request to be near to Him never falls on deaf ears.

❯ EXPLORE THE TEXT

READ THE BIBLE: Ask a volunteer to read Psalm 42.

DISCUSS: Use the following questions to discuss group members' initial reactions to the text.

> What immediately stands out to you in this text as a theme or primary point? What do you find encouraging, timely, or convicting?

> What can we conclude from verse 1? What are the primary causes of spiritual droughts today?

> What kinds of problems arise today, both inside and outside the church, when people attempt to quench their thirst for God with other things?

> How did the psalmist ultimately respond to his feelings of despair and his sense of isolation from God? What lessons can we apply when we face despair and feel distant from the Lord?

> What else does this text teach us about God? About ourselves?

> What other questions or observations do you have?

NOTE: Provide ample time for group members to share responses and questions about the text. Don't feel pressured to prioritize the printed agenda over group members' personal experiences. If time allows, discuss responses to the questions in the personal reading.

❯ OBEY THE TEXT

RESPOND: Foster an environment of openness and action. Help individuals apply biblical truth to specific areas of personal thought, attitude, and/or behavior.

> In what ways do you typically respond to suffering? Do your reactions point people to the presence of God? What practices can you put into place so that you always direct people to God's faithfulness, even when you're enduring hardships?

PRAY: Close by praying for enduring hope in God's presence, even when He seems far away.

❯ TIPS FOR LEADING A GROUP

PRAYERFULLY PREPARE

Prepare for each session by—

> ❯ **reviewing the weekly material and group questions ahead of time;**
> ❯ **praying for each person in the group.**

Ask the Holy Spirit to work through you and the group discussion to help people take steps toward Jesus each week as directed by God's Word.

MINIMIZE DISTRACTIONS

Create a comfortable environment. If group members are uncomfortable, they'll be distracted and therefore not engaged in the group experience. Plan ahead by taking into consideration—

> ❯ **seating;**
> ❯ **temperature;**
> ❯ **lighting;**
> ❯ **food or drink;**
> ❯ **surrounding noise;**
> ❯ **general cleanliness (put pets away if meeting in a home).**

At best, thoughtfulness and hospitality show guests and group members they're welcome and valued in whatever environment you choose to gather. At worst, people may never notice your effort, but they're also not distracted. Do everything in your ability to help people focus on what's most important: connecting with God, with the Bible, and with others.

INCLUDE OTHERS

Your goal is to foster a community in which people are welcome just as they are but encouraged to grow spiritually. Always be aware of opportunities to—

> ❯ **invite** new people to join your group;
> ❯ **include** any people who visit the group.

An inexpensive way to make first-time guests feel welcome or to invite people to get involved is to give them their own copies of this Bible-study book.

ENCOURAGE DISCUSSION

A good small group has the following characteristics.

> **Everyone participates.** Encourage everyone to ask questions, share responses, or read aloud.

> **No one dominates—not even the leader.** Be sure what you say takes up less than half of your time together as a group. Politely redirect discussion if anyone dominates.

> **Nobody is rushed through questions.** Don't feel that a moment of silence is a bad thing. People often need time to think about their responses to questions they've just heard or to gain courage to share what God is stirring in their hearts.

> **Input is affirmed and followed up.** Make sure you point out something true or helpful in a response. Don't just move on. Build personal connections with follow-up questions, asking how other people have experienced similar things or how a truth has shaped their understanding of God and the Scripture you're studying. People are less likely to speak up if they fear that you don't actually want to hear their answers or that you're looking for only a certain answer.

> **God and His Word are central.** Opinions and experiences can be helpful, but God has given us the truth. Trust Scripture to be the authority and God's Spirit to work in people's lives. You can't change anyone, but God can. Continually point people to the Word and to active steps of faith.

KEEP CONNECTING

Think of ways to connect with members during the week. Participation during the session is always improved when members spend time connecting with one another away from the session. The more people are comfortable with and involved in one another's lives, the more they'll look forward to being together. When people move beyond being friendly and in the same group to truly being friends who form a community, they come to each session eager to engage instead of merely attending.

Encourage group members with thoughts, commitments, or questions from the session by connecting through—

> **emails;**
> **texts;**
> **social media.**

When possible, build deeper friendships by planning or spontaneously inviting group members to join you outside your regularly scheduled group time for—

> **meals;**
> **fun activities;**
> **projects around your home, church, or community.**

❯GROUP CONTACT INFORMATION

Name _____ Number _____
Email/social media _____

Name _____ Number _____
Email/social media _____

Name _____ Number _____
Email/social media _____

Name _____ Number _____
Email/social media _____

Name _____ Number _____
Email/social media _____

Name _____ Number _____
Email/social media _____

Name _____ Number _____
Email/social media _____

Name _____ Number _____
Email/social media _____

Name _____ Number _____
Email/social media _____

Name _____ Number _____
Email/social media _____

Name _____ Number _____
Email/social media _____